FORTRESS • 85

SCAPA FLOW

The defences of Britain's great fleet anchorage
1914–45

ANGUS KONSTAM

ILLUSTRATED BY PETER DENNIS

Series editors Marcus Cowper and Nikolai Bogdanovic

First published in 2009 by Osprey Publishing
Midland House, West Way, Botley, Oxford OX2 0PH, UK
443 Park Avenue South, New York, NY 10016, USA
E-mail: info@ospreypublishing.com

ISBN 978 1 84603 366 7
E-book ISBN 978 1 84908 082 8

Editorial by Ilios Publishing, Oxford, UK (www.iliospublishing.com)
Page layout by Ken Vail Graphic Design, Cambridge, UK (kvgd.com)
Cartography: Map Studio, Romsey, UK
Index by Alison Worthington
Originated by PDQ Digital Media Solutions, Bungay, UK
Printed in China through Bookbuilders

09 10 11 12   10 9 8 7 6 5 4 3 2 1

A CIP catalogue record for this book is available from the British Library.

FOR A CATALOGUE OF ALL BOOKS PUBLISHED BY OSPREY MILITARY
AND AVIATION PLEASE CONTACT:

Osprey Direct, c/o Random House Distribution Center,
400 Hahn Road, Westminster, MD 21157
E-mail: uscustomerservice@ospreypublishing.com

Osprey Direct, The Book Service Ltd, Distribution Centre,
Colchester Road, Frating Green, Colchester, Essex, CO7 7DW
E-mail: customerservice@ospreypublishing.com

www.ospreypublishing.com

DEDICATION

To my mother, Dr Sheila T. Konstam, whose house overlooks Scapa Bay.

ARTIST'S NOTE

Readers may care to note that the original paintings from which the colour plates in this book were prepared are available for private sale. All reproduction copyright whatsoever is retained by the Publishers. All enquiries should be addressed to:

Peter Dennis, Fieldhead, The Park, Mansfield, Notts, NG18 2AT, UK

The Publishers regret that they can enter into no correspondence upon this matter.

THE FORTRESS STUDY GROUP (FSG)

The object of the FSG is to advance the education of the public in the study of all aspects of fortifications and their armaments, especially works constructed to mount or resist artillery. The FSG holds an annual conference in September over a long weekend with visits and evening lectures, an annual tour abroad lasting about eight days, and an annual Members' Day.

The FSG journal FORT is published annually, and its newsletter Casemate is published three times a year. Membership is international. For further details, please contact:

The Secretary, c/o 6 Lanark Place, London W9 1BS, UK

Website: www.fsgfort.com

THE WOODLAND TRUST

Osprey Publishing are supporting the Woodland Trust, the UK's leading woodland conservation charity, by funding the dedication of trees.

CONTENTS

SCAPA FLOW: THE DEFENCES OF BRITAIN'S GREAT FLEET ANCHORAGE

The reason for the defences: the battlecruiser HMS *Hood*, lying at anchor in Scapa Flow, photographed from beneath the guns of another capital ship shortly before the outbreak of World War II. The vessel on the far left is the battlecruiser HMS *Renown*. (Stratford Archive)

INTRODUCTION

During the two great conflicts of the 20th century the natural harbour of Scapa Flow served as Britain's main naval base, and consequently it was a place of immense strategic importance. It was from Scapa that the Royal Navy sallied to do battle with the German High Seas Fleet in 1916, and in World War II British warships left this safe haven to hunt down the *Bismarck* and the *Scharnhorst*. Even though it lay far from any enemy-occupied ports, Scapa was the cornerstone of Britain's defences in both wars, providing a secure base that helped the Royal Navy maintain its control of the seas.

Scapa Flow lies in the middle of Orkney, an archipelago lying just off the north-eastern tip of Scotland. The largest of these islands, known by Orcadians as the Mainland, protects the northern half of the anchorage, while to the south a string of smaller islands encircles Scapa Flow like a green necklace. The largest of these is Hoy, a sparsely inhabited island whose heather-covered hills and rough moorland is unlike the rest of Orkney, which presents a more pleasing and fertile landscape. In fact, in good weather Orkney can be a place of incredible beauty, with clear blue seas, lush green fields and an almost magical

Lyness Naval Base, photographed from the summit of Wee Fea Hill. The base contained a naval headquarters, communications centres, a major fuel depot, a boom defence workshop, repair workshops, stores and recreational facilities. (Private collection)

light. By contrast an Orkney winter can be bleak, cold and miserable. For tens of thousands of servicemen during two world wars, Orkney must have seemed like the end of the earth, a far-flung corner of Britain that was completely removed from anywhere they had ever encountered. This explains the love-hate relationship these servicemen had with their wartime home.

Of course, this vital naval base had to be defended. This meant covering its approaches with coastal batteries, stationing troops in Orkney to repel an enemy landing, and the blocking of entrances using booms, anti-submarine nets, blockships and other obstacles. In World War II the defenders faced the new threat of air attack, and so Scapa Flow was eventually ringed by anti-aircraft batteries and searchlight stations, and protected by fighter aircraft based on Orkney airfields. The result of all this was to create one of the most extensive integrated land, sea and air defence systems of World War II, a near impregnable base that allowed the Royal Navy to perform its task without worrying about the safety of its own anchorage. However, all this took time to create, and in both world wars the Germans launched attacks on Scapa Flow before these defences were complete. In 1939 one such attack by a U-boat resulted in the sinking of a British battleship, anchored inside the seemingly impregnable defensive cordon. This book tells the story of these defences, and of the men who manned them.

First though, we need to explain the meaning of the name. In the 8th century AD Orkney was colonized by the Vikings, and consequently many Norse words found their way into the Orkney lexicon. 'Scapa' comes from the Norse word *skalpr* (a poetic term for a longboat), and *skalpei* (ship isthmus – a place where ships could be hauled over a short stretch of land). Scapa Bay is one and a quarter miles (two kilometres) away from the waters of Kirkwall Bay, and the flat valley between the two bays forms a natural isthmus that the Vikings would have used in this way. 'Flow' comes from the Norse word *flot*, meaning a substantial body of water, or a wide fjord. That seems a perfect description for the 'Flow'.

Finally, as an author I've written dozens of books for Osprey, including three titles in this Fortress series. However, *Scapa Flow* is special. Although I wasn't born in Orkney (I arrived there when I was three), I was brought up in the islands and as a 'peedie' (little) boy I explored the derelict pillboxes and gun emplacements, or scrambled over the blockships and barriers. My bedroom windows overlooked Scapa Bay, and I was brought up amid the constant reminders of the part played by Orkney in two world wars. Consequently this book has given me great pleasure to research and write.

CHRONOLOGY

1812 Scapa Flow first recommended to the Admiralty as a 'rendezvous base' for warships.

1816 Completion of first fortifications designed to protect Scapa Flow.

1860 Orkney Royal Garrison Artillery formed, and volunteers trained in coastal gunnery.

1898 British Channel Fleet used Orkney as a base during its summer manoeuvres.

1905 First Sea Lord Jackie Fisher recommends Scapa Flow be turned into a naval base.

1908 HMS *Triton* conducts extensive survey of Scapa Flow for the Admiralty.

1910 The Grand Fleet uses Scapa Flow as a temporary base. First modern coastal guns enter service in Orkney batteries.

1913 War Office turns control of the nascent Scapa Flow officially designated as a major naval base.

1914
June First elements of the Grand Fleet sent to Scapa Flow.

August Outbreak of World War I. Naval guns landed from fleet to bolster defences.

September U-boat scare prompts fleet to put to sea until defences can be improved.

November Work begins on coastal defence batteries overlooking main entrances.

1915
February Anti-submarine nets put in place, followed by anti-shipping booms.

April 19 'blockships' scuttled across the eastern entrances of Scapa Flow.

July 'Indicator loops' and minefields laid around Hoxa Sound and Hoy Sound. King George V visits Scapa Flow.

1916
30 May Grand Fleet sails from Scapa Flow to make contact with the German fleet.

31 May Battle of Jutland.

5 June HMS *Hampshire* sunk by mine off Marwick Head, Orkney, claiming the life of Field Marshal Lord Kitchener.

1917
9 July The battleship HMS *Vanguard* blows up at her moorings in Scapa Flow.

1917
December US 6th Battle Squadron joins the Royal Navy in Scapa Flow.

1918
28 October *UB-116* sunk in Hoxa Sound.

11 November Armistice. End of World War I.

23 November The German High Seas Fleet is interned in Scapa Flow.

1919
23 June Scuttling of the High Sea Fleet – 52 warships sunk by their own crews.

1920 Scapa Flow ceases to be a naval base.

February
1924–39 Salvage of the German fleet by commercial salvors.

1938 Scapa Flow designated as a 'Category A' defended port. 'Munich crisis' prompts the commissioning of work on coastal batteries.

1939
3 September Outbreak of World War II. Orkney Territorial Army units occupy Scapa Flow defences.

29 September Orkney and Shetland Defence Force (OSDef) established.

13 October Penetration of Scapa Flow by U-47 – sinking of HMS *Royal Oak*.

17 October First Luftwaffe air attack on Scapa Flow. HMS *Iron Duke* damaged.

1940
February RAF Airfields in Orkney become operational.

March Defences now consist of eight coastal batteries, 50 AA guns, and 10,000 troops. Home Fleet returns to Scapa Flow after anti-submarine defences strengthened.

11 March Churchill reports to War Cabinet that Scapa Flow is now '80% secure'.

16 March Second Luftwaffe raid on Scapa Flow – first Orcadian civilian casualty.

2 April First use of the new 'Orkney Barrage' proves a resounding success.

8 April	Third and largest Luftwaffe raid on Scapa Flow. Germans invade Denmark and Norway.
10 April	Fourth Luftwaffe raid on Scapa flow.
May	Construction begins on the Churchill Barriers.
June	All coastal guns and AA batteries now in position around Scapa Flow.
1941	
March	Scapa Flow defences reach their peak of strength and effectiveness.
7 March	Gunther Prien and crew of *U-47* sunk during attack on convoy.
21 May	Elements of Home Fleet (including HMS *Hood*) leave Scapa Flow during operations against the *Bismarck*.
22 June	Germany attacks the Soviet Union.
August	Commencement of Arctic convoys.
10 October	First homebound Arctic convoy arrives in Scapa Flow.
7 December	United States enters the war.
1942	
1–13 July	Attack on Convoy PQ-17.
November	Churchill Barriers now effectively seal off the eastern approaches to Scapa Flow.
1943	
May 1943	Turning point of the Battle of the Atlantic – 41 U-boats lost in one month.
June	First reduction in garrison strength. Many searchlight batteries withdrawn.
26 December	*Scharnhorst* sunk in the battle of North Cape.
1944	
1 January	*Duke of York* returns to Scapa Flow after her victory against the *Scharnhorst*.
February	Withdrawal of heavy AA guns and garrison infantry amid D-Day preparations.
1945	
March	Naval base reduced in status as Admiral commanding hauls down his flag.
8 May	VE Day – peace in Europe.
12 May	Churchill Barriers officially opened to traffic.
June–July	Major reductions in garrison strength.
15 August	VJ Day – end of war with Japan.

THE DEVELOPMENT OF SCAPA FLOW'S DEFENCES

The potential of Scapa Flow as a maritime anchorage was first recognized a century before World War I. At the outbreak of the War of 1812 an Orkney-born maritime surveyor called Graeme Spence suggested to the Admiralty that the land-ringed natural harbour would make an excellent 'rendezvous base' for Royal Naval warships engaged as convoy escorts. At the time French and American privateers were preying on merchant shipping, and Scapa Flow was already used as a gathering point for convoys bound for Sweden. Following Spence's recommendation the anchorage at Lyness was protected by the building of two Martello towers, but work was completed on these defences only after the onset of peace.

The naval potential of Scapa Flow was forgotten. However, the pattern of European war was changing, and if Germany rather than France was the new enemy, then Orkney was better placed as a base than either Portsmouth or Plymouth. During the first decade of the 20th century the Admiralty debated the strategic consequences of a German war, and the location of the Navy's principal naval base if war were declared. Scapa Flow was a virtually land-locked area of water, with narrow entrance channels that were further protected by tides and shoals. Set against this were the problems of supply, transport of men and stores, and the general lack of infrastructure. Turning Scapa Flow into a defended anchorage for the British Grand Fleet would present the Admiralty with a major logistical problem.

Other sites were also considered, including the Cromarty Firth and the Firth of Forth on the east coast of Scotland, and the Humber Estuary in the north of England. However, all these locations were vulnerable, as they could be easily blocked by mines. Only Scapa Flow had more than one entrance, and it would be almost impossible for an enemy to block both main entrances at the same time. In 1919 Admiral 'Jackie' Fisher declared that it was he who had 'discovered' Scapa Flow during his tenure as First Sea Lord:

Looking at a chart in the secluded room in the Admiralty, in 1905, I saw a large landlocked sheet of water, unsurveyed and nameless. It was Scapa Flow. One hour after this an Admiralty survey ship was en route there. Secretly she went, for none but myself and my most excellent friend the hydrographer knew. No one, however talented except myself, could explain how, playing with one leg of the compasses I swept the chart with the other leg, to find a place for our fleet beyond the practicability of surprise by the Germans. The fleet was there in Scapa Flow before the war broke out.

Survey teams became regular visitors to the islands during the decade before the outbreak of World War I, inspecting sites where coastal defence batteries could be placed or laying out potential anchorages. The fleet was also a regular visitor to Orkney, as Scapa Flow became a temporary anchorage during fleet exercises. The local Volunteers (who reluctantly became part of the Territorial Army in 1908) were trained in gunnery, and were therefore destined to man any coastal defences once they were installed. They were duly named the Orkney Royal Garrison Artillery (Territorial), and the Orcadian volunteers prided themselves on the importance of their role in any future conflict. However, no defences were built before the war began.

World War I

When war was declared in August 1914, Scapa Flow was a naval base in name only. It boasted no defensive coastal batteries or protective minefields, no booms to seal the entrances off to enemy U-boats, and no shore facilities

In 1914 no guns were available to protect Scapa Flow, so as a stopgap a handful of pieces were ordered from America. Consequently in 1915 this American-built 5.5in. QF gun was installed in Ness Battery No. 2, overlooking Hoy Sound. (Stratford Archive)

During 1914 Admiral Jellicoe ordered that a number of guns be landed from the fleet to provide a stopgap form of coastal defence for the anchorage. In this photograph sailors man a 3-pdr QF piece mounted at Innan Neb, Flotta, which covered Switha Sound. (Stratford Archive)

to provide logistical or domestic support to the fleet. All of this would have to be created.

Admiral Sir John Jellicoe, who had just taken over command of the Grand Fleet, declared himself to be appalled at the lack of defences. He did what he could by landing small ships' guns, and placing them in temporary batteries that covered Hoxa Sound and Hoy Sound – the two main entrances to Scapa Flow.

These meagre defences were augmented by destroyer patrols, mounted off both main entrances, while old merchant ships were purchased, ready to be used as blockships to seal the smaller eastern entrances to Scapa Flow. Fishing nets were hung from buoys, and strung across Hoxa Sound and Hoy Sound, serving as a primitive form of anti-submarine barrier. Jellicoe hoped that these makeshift defensive measures would deter the Germans until proper defences could be put in their place.

In August 1914 the main fleet anchorage was established in Scapa Bay, the northern part of Scapa Flow closest to the islands' main town of Kirkwall, while the base headquarters was established at Scapa Pier. Three months later the base was relocated to the small village of Longhope, on Hoy, while the fleet anchorage was moved to the waters off the island of Flotta, on the southern side of Scapa Flow. After a brief inter-service argument the Admiralty took over control of Orkney's nascent coastal defences from the Royal Garrison Artillery – a force that was largely made up of the gunnery of the local Territorial Army. Consequently the Orcadian gunners found themselves surplus to requirements and, despite a very vocal protest, they were disbanded and dispersed to other artillery units within the Territorial Army. It was a lesson in military intransigence that the Orcadians were slow to forget.

However, the most immediate danger facing the fleet was the threat posed by U-boats rather than an invasion force or a raid by the German fleet. On 9 August the war was barely a week old when the cruiser HMS *Birmingham* spotted *U-15* on the surface, between Orkney and Fair Isle. The quick-thinking commander rammed and sank the U-boat before she could submerge, and *U-15* went down with all hands. In September the fleet was thrown into a panic when it was thought that a U-boat had successfully navigated its way into Scapa Flow, and in 'The First Battle of Scapa Flow' nervous gunners fired at anything they thought might be a periscope, including seals and seabirds. Jellicoe responded by keeping his fleet at sea for long periods, so that something could be done to improve the anti-submarine defences of the anchorage.

Unloading coal supplies for the garrison at Stanger Head, Flotta, during World War I. The coastal battery at Stanger Head was sited on top of a cliff, so the best way to transport food, fuel, stores and ammunition to the battery was by boat and crane. (Orkney Library & Archives)

A 6in. QF Mark IV, one of two such pieces mounted on Hoxa Head during World War I. They covered Hoxa Sound, the main entrance into Scapa Flow, and with an effective range of 13,700m (15,000 yards) they would have been highly effective weapons. (Orkney Library & Archives)

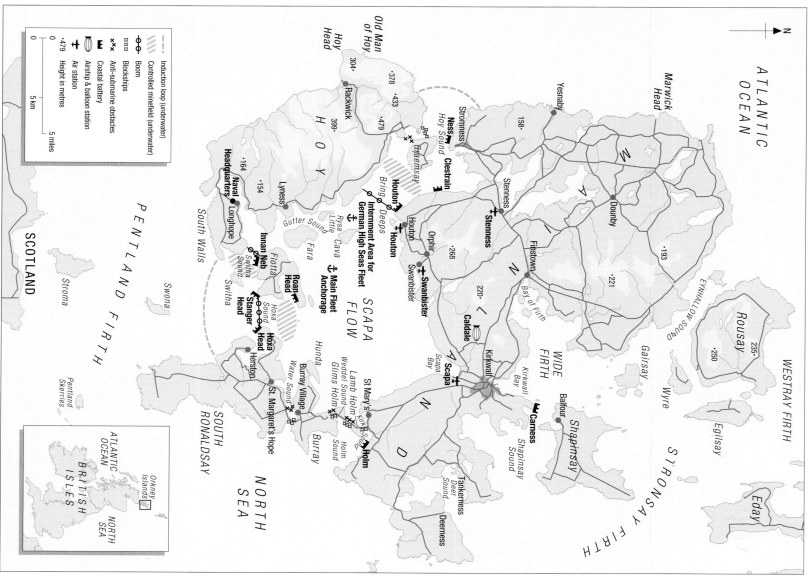

The defences of Scapa Flow during World War I

The first problem was to seal off the narrow entrances on the eastern side of Scapa Flow, which lay between the Orkney Mainland and the smaller islands of Lamb Holm, Glims Holm, Burray and South Ronaldsay. The simple and reasonably effective solution was to sink 15 old merchant ships in the four channels: four in Kirk Sound between the Mainland near the village of Holm and the island of Lamb Holm, five in Skerry Sound between Lamb Holm and Glims Holm, three in Weddel Sound between Glims Holm and Burray, and finally three in Water Sound between the two largest islands in the chain – Burray and South Ronaldsay. These 'blockships' sealed off the channels to enemy U-boats – and to local fishing boats.

Five more blockships were sunk in Burra Sound, between the north-east corner of Hoy and the island of Graemsay. Behind the line of blockships a number of steel anti-submarine obstacles were placed in the shallower channels. In effect these blockships and other obstacles reduced the number of entrances to Scapa Flow from eight down to just three – Hoy Sound, Hoxa Sound and its smaller neighbour Switha Sound.

Two types of boom sealed these three waterways. The first was an anti-shipping boom, designed to deter an attack by enemy destroyers. Wooden boxes were chained together, forming a pliable but stout barrier. Boom vessels (converted drifters) were employed to open and close the boom for friendly ships. One of these booms ran across Hoxa Sound between Hoxa Head and Stanger Head, and was in place by December 1914. The second was sited at the back of Hoy Sound, spanning the Bring Deeps between Houton on the Mainland and Scad Head on Hoy; a third barrier protected Switha Sound, and lay between Inman Neb on Flotta and South Walls on Hoy. These last two booms were in place by February 1915. The theory behind these booms was that a fast-moving destroyer would suffer extensive damage if it hit them, allowing the shore batteries that covered the booms to pound the enemy warship with 4in. and 12-pdr shells. Even if the boom broke the attack would be slowed down or halted long enough for the gunners to do their work. A fourth boom covered the approaches to Kirkwall Bay.

An anti-submarine net also protected each of the three main entrances. By the summer of 1915 the first makeshift nets had been replaced by purpose-built steel nets. Lookout posts and searchlight positions were also established along the shore, and hydrophone listening stations were established in all the principal gun batteries. A defensive minefield was laid off Hoy Sound, while controlled minefields were placed in all three entrance channels. By the middle of 1915 these had been augmented by 'induction loops' – magnetically charged cables laid along the seabed. The idea was that a submerged U-boat would cause a significant fluctuation in the magnetic charge, which could be detected by an operator watching a dial in a shore station. In effect it worked as an early warning device for enemy submersibles.

These induction loops were laid across the entrance to Hoxa and Switha sounds, and in the western approaches to Hoy Sound. Once an enemy U-boat was detected then a warning would be given to gunners, searchlight operators and warships in the area. Then, when the U-boat reached one of the three

main entrances, it would pass over a 'guard loop', which was a smaller version of an induction loop. Beyond these guard loops lay the controlled minefields, which could be activated by an operator on the shore. By flicking a switch he could arm the mines, and the U-boat would inevitably collide with one. The system was tried only once in anger, in the closing weeks of the war, and it worked with deadly efficiency.

Then there were the coastal batteries, covering all three channels, as well as the narrower Lamb Sound on the eastern side of the Flow, and the entrance into Kirkwall Bay, which by then was established as the base for the Northern Patrol, which patrolled the waters between Britain and Iceland looking for enemy or neutral ships trying to run the blockade into German ports. Hoy Sound was defended by two groups of batteries. The first was the Ness Battery, sited just to the west of Stromness, the second-largest town in Orkney. In September 1914 Jellicoe ordered the installation of a temporary battery, consisting of two 12-pdr Quick Fire (QF) guns, taken from a warship. By the end of the year another two 12-pdrs had been installed on the Point of Ness.

When the war began the Admiralty found itself short of suitable guns to defend the anchorage, so several pieces were ordered from the Bethlehem Steel Company of Pennsylvania. By the spring of 1915 the first of these guns had arrived, and they were installed in three battery positions at Ness. Battery 1 at Outertown and Battery 2 on the sloping ground nearer the shore both contained

Steel anti-submarine obstacles were erected across some of the shallower channels leading into Scapa Flow during World War I. This structure was sited in Burra Sound, between Graemsay and the north-east corner of Hoy. (Orkney Library & Archives)

two 6in. guns apiece. Battery 3, located between Battery 2 and the Point of Ness contained three 5.5in. guns. Orkney Territorial crews served these smaller guns, while Royal Marine gunners crewed the larger pieces. Once these new guns were operational the 12-pdrs were removed and sent to augment the Clestrain Battery.

While the Ness batteries covered the approaches to Hoy Sound, the Clestrain and Houton batteries dominated the far end of it, where it entered Scapa Flow. Houton was where the boom spanned the channel, and to cover it two 12-pdr QF guns were installed on the steep headland, which was then crowned by a small signal station. The battery was operational in the spring of 1915. Until then Hoy Sound was covered by the 9in. and 6in. guns of HMS *Crescent*. When the 12-pdrs were removed from the Ness Battery it was decided to use them in Clestrain, and by the autumn of 1915 the Clestrain Battery was fully operational.

Hoxa Sound was protected by three batteries, on Stanger Head, Roan Head and Hoxa Head. Stanger Head was the first battery to become operational, when four 12-pdr QF guns were installed there in September 1914. By the spring of 1915 these stopgap pieces were removed, and replaced by four 4in. QF guns, in two adjacent twin batteries. Later that year two American-built 6in. guns were installed in their own battery, a few hundred metres to the west of the 4in. gun emplacements, and just in front of the naval signalling station which controlled shipping movements in and out of the Sound.

In early 1915 three small 3-pdr QF guns were mounted at Roan Head, on the north-eastern tip of Flotta. Later in the war these small guns were replaced by more effective 12-pdr pieces, taken from the Holm Battery.

In March 1915 four 4in. QF guns were installed at Hoxa Head in South Ronaldsay, which lay on the eastern side of Hoxa Sound. The guns were mounted in twin batteries, the design of which mirrored those of the Ness and Stanger batteries. Together with their counterparts on Stanger Head just under a mile away, they covered the boom which spanned Hoxa Sound. In May 1916 an additional battery was created, this time on the southern tip of the headland. The two 6in. QF guns mounted there were designed to cover the southern approaches to Hoxa Sound and Switha Sound, just like the similar large calibre guns on Stanger Head.

Switha Sound was a smaller, narrow channel, which was infrequently used, but with a depth of 11 fathoms (66ft, 20m) it provided the smaller ships of the fleet with direct access to the Naval HQ at Longhope. It was protected by the battery on Innan Neb in Flotta, which was usually referred to simply as the Neb Battery. In September 1914 two 3-pdrs were landed from a warship and installed there, but in late 1915 these small pieces were replaced

NESS BATTERY NO. 3, STROMNESS, 1916

This battery, built to defend the western entrance into Scapa Flow through Hoy Sound was typical of the gun batteries built to defend the anchorage. Each of the three 5.5in. breech-loading (BL) guns (1) was housed in its own concrete emplacement, flanked by small expenditure magazines. Ammunition was housed in an underground magazine (2), approached through trenches lined with dry-stone walling.

The Ness Battery consisted of three gun positions, sited as shown in the inset. Battery No. 3 was sited overlooking the foreshore, while the other two batteries lay further inland. All these guns had a maximum range of c.13,700m (15,000 yards).

by two 4.7in. QF guns, mounted in what had become the standard type of battery – two or more guns in concrete emplacements, served by a single underground magazine reached by means of two cuttings. The guns were sited to cover the boom that stretched across Switha Sound.

One other battery protected the smallest entrance into Scapa Flow – Kirk Sound – which was accessible to small boats willing to weave their way through the anti-submarine obstacles and blockships. In late 1914 four 12-pdr QF guns were emplaced on the shore of Holm parish, near the rock outcrop known as the Tower of Clett. The guns were sited to cover Holm Sound to the east, and Kirk Sound directly in front of the guns, which ran between the Holm mainland and the small island of Lamb Holm. In early 1916 the guns were removed, and three of them were moved to Roan Head in Flotta. They were replaced at Holm by three 4in. pieces.

The only other battery in Orkney was at the Point of Carness, which guarded the entrance into Kirkwall Bay, and covered the Kirkwall boom, which stretched between Carness and Helliar Holm, a small island on the far side of The String, the main shipping channel between the Orkney Mainland and the island of Shapinsay. It is a little unclear exactly what guns were mounted here, as accounts vary, but the likelihood is that they were two 4in. QF pieces. All the batteries mentioned above were surrounded by all the supporting structures they needed to function properly – battery observation posts, searchlight positions close to the shore, magazines, barracks, mess halls, kitchens, ablution blocks, stores and battery headquarters offices. Each was virtually a self-contained army camp, although together they formed a cordon which protected the fleet sheltering behind the batteries.

Another feature of the protection afforded to Scapa Flow during World War I was that as well as defences on land and sea, it involved defence in the air. In 1914 aircraft were in their infancy, and air warfare had yet to be invented. Orkney was the scene of some of the first experiments in naval aviation, and during the war it played host to a growing and vibrant air defence force. The first taste of this new form of warfare came in September 1914, when a cattle boat unloaded two aircraft onto Scapa Pier – both seaplanes – of the newly formed Royal Naval Air Service (RNAS). Another three followed, including two land-based planes. These were deposited in a field at the head of Scapa Bay, and in time the site grew into Orkney's first air station.

An equally precarious form of air reconnaissance was provided by kite balloons, and in 1916 work started on the construction of a kite balloon station at Houton, which also had a seaplane base attached to it. In many cases these balloons were towed from converted drifters or merchant ships, and the observers were used to detect mines or U-boats. Given that Orkney during winter was notorious for its high winds, this was a dangerous business. One airman recalled that 'one gusty day a balloon broke free. The last unfortunate man to hold on to his guy rope was carried up 30 feet, and fell,

Royal Marine gunners, pictured in front of the cliffs of Stanger Head on Flotta during World War I. Their dress is typical of the winter clothing worn by the men of the coastal defence batteries during the war. (Orkney Library & Archives)

injuring his spine. I was ordered to chase the balloon on my motorcycle, to report where it went to.' When last spotted the balloon was heading northwards from Orkney 'and making excellent progress'.

Another form of balloon that saw service as an anti-submarine device was the airship. In July 1916 the Caldale Airship Station entered service on the outskirts of Kirkwall, and two large hangars were built to house two 'Submarine Scout' (SS) airships. These craft were 44m long, and their 75hp engines gave them an average speed of 80km/ph (50mph). The plan was to use them for anti-submarine and mine-spotting sweeps around Orkney, but it was soon found that strong headwinds often made flying difficult. Then in November 1917 the engine of the SSP-2 failed during a gale, and she was lost at sea. Just a week later another airship – the SSP-4 – crashed into the sea off Westray, and her three-man crew were never recovered. These fatal accidents, plus a string of wrecks caused by landings in high winds, caused the Admiralty to move their remaining airships back down to the south of England, where the weather was more conducive. By January 1918 Caldale had become a kite balloon repair station.

However, the seaplanes used by the Royal Naval Air Service proved a great success, and soon a subsidiary air station was created in the south-east corner of Stenness Loch. Unfortunately the shallow water of the sea loch proved unsuitable for sustained operations, and although the base became operational in 1918, it was rarely used. Another seaplane station at Swanbister in Orphir was never completed by the time the war ended. Scapa eventually became a seaplane repair base.

With its base secure, the Navy had little to do but wait for the Germans to make a move. While the smaller ships of the fleet conducted patrols, or hunted for enemy U-boats, the rest of the fleet spent much of the time at anchor inside Scapa Flow, where boredom appeared a far greater enemy than the German fleet. Then, on 30 May 1916, Jellicoe learned that the German High Seas Fleet had put to sea. That evening some 72 warships of the Grand Fleet passed through Hoxa Sound. The two fleets clashed off the Danish coast during the following afternoon (31 May). This long-awaited fleet engagement – the battle of Jutland – ended with the Germans returning to port, allowing the British to claim a victory of sorts. The real victory was a strategic one: the German fleet never returned to sea, and the Royal Navy continued to dominate the North Sea.

Within days of the fleet's return to Scapa Flow another warship was lost. Field Marshal Lord Kitchener, Minister of War and former colonial general was a familiar face thanks to the recruiting poster where he exhorted 'Your Country Needs You.' In early June he was sent to Russia to meet with the Russian High Command. On 5 June he had lunch with Jellicoe on board his flagship HMS *Iron Duke*, then transferred to the armoured cruiser HMS *Hampshire*. That evening she passed through Hoxa Sound, and steamed around the western side of Orkney. A full gale was blowing, and her destroyer escorts were sent back into port. At around 10pm the cruiser struck a mine as she passed Marwick Head. She sank in less than 15 minutes, taking Kitchener and all but 12 of her 655-man crew down with her.

Because of the gale the western approaches to Orkney had not been swept for mines for several days. The Germans later claimed credit for the disaster, as just over a week before *U-75* commanded by Korvettenkapitän Kurt Beitzen had laid 34 mines in the area. While conspiracy theories abounded, the likelihood is that the *Hampshire* was simply in the wrong place that night.

Another disaster overtook the fleet the following year, when on 9 July 1917 the battleship HMS *Vanguard* blew up at her moorings. At the time she was anchored off Flotta. Just before midnight there was a tremendous explosion, and lookouts on other ships watched in horror as the battleship was ripped apart. According to an eyewitness a trawler that was close by got smothered in blood and pieces of human flesh. One gun turret was blown onto the nearby shore. Of the 846 men on board that night, there were only three survivors.

While these tragedies were rare events, there were other naval losses. In February 1915 the destroyers HMS *Goldfinch* and HMS *Sparrowhawk* ran aground off Start Point on Sanday, and although the latter vessel was refloated, *Goldfinch* was a complete wreck. Fortunately no lives were lost. Three years later in January 1918 the destroyers HMS *Opal* and HMS *Narborough* ran into the cliffs on the eastern side of South Ronaldsay during a snowstorm. Of almost 200 men on board the two ships, there was only one survivor. A more cheerful event was the arrival of a squadron of the US Navy. However, like their British counterparts, they spent the last year of the war waiting for a German sortie that never took place.

Between the wars

The Armistice of 11 November 1918 brought the war to an end, and with it came the promise of relief for the thousands of servicemen whose war had been spent in Scapa Flow. As well as the long-awaited reward of demobilization, peace also witnessed the arrival of the German High Seas Fleet. The German fleet had surrendered, and a total of 74 German disarmed warships were duly interned in the anchorage.The bulk of their crews were soon repatriated to Germany, but 1,700 remained, under the command of Admiral von Reuter. It was a miserable time for these German sailors, far from home, facing an uncertain future. Indiscipline was rife, forcing the Admiral to move his flagship from the battleship *Friedrich der Grosse* to the light cruiser *Emden*, whose crew were considered less mutinous than most. While most of the Royal Navy ships returned to their home ports and the shore batteries were dismantled, the German fleet remained in limbo – the victims of the drawn-out peace negotiations at Versailles. Then in May 1919 Reuter learned the harsh terms of the peace treaty that was being negotiated. The fleet would be divided between the Allies, while the strength of the German Navy would be reduced to a skeleton force of 16,500 men, with no U-boats and precious few capital ships. The admiral decided to deny the enemy this last great prize.

The Treaty of Versailles was due to be signed on Saturday 21 June, although in fact its signature was delayed by two days. Reuter had planned his protest with great efficiency. That Saturday morning, following a pre-arranged signal from the *Emden*, the German crews began scuttling their ships. At 10.40am the men on the handful of Royal Navy guardships noticed something was amiss. One officer recalled: 'I was standing on the deck of the *Victorious* when I noticed a number of small boats pushing off from the

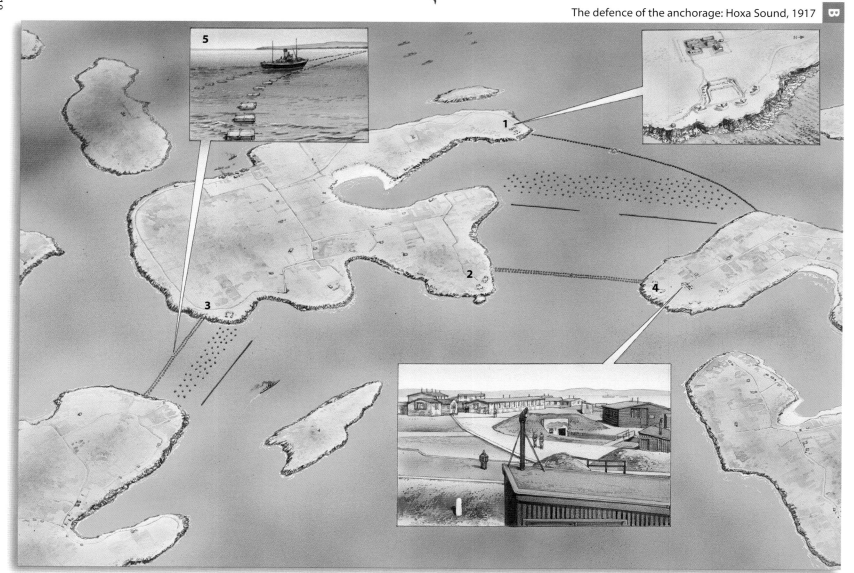

B THE DEFENCE OF THE ANCHORAGE: HOXA SOUND, 1917

The main southern entrance into Scapa Flow was through Hoxa Sound between the island of Flotta and Hoxa Head, on South Ronaldsay. Another smaller entrance – Switha Sound – lay on the south-western side of Flotta. Both entrances were covered by gun batteries, at Roan Head (**1**), Stanger Head (**2**) and Innan Neb (**3**) on Flotta, and on Hoxa Head (**4**). Each camp was supported by a small encampment, which housed the gunners and their stores. These were augmented by searchlight positions and by lookout posts. Anti-ship and anti-submarine booms were stretched across both entrances (**5**), operated by drifters. A series of hydrophone listening posts and magnetic induction loops (solid red lines) were designed to detect enemy submarines, and controlled minefields (red dots) could be detonated from the shore. Hoxa Sound was further defended by a second boom, behind the controlled minefield.

German ships. In minutes the German flags were hoisted on the ships, and then as in a dream of fantasy I saw them moving. Some wobbled, some rolled over on their sides, many sank stern or bows first, the lighter craft sank squarely; many were enveloped in clouds of steam.' By late afternoon 52 German warships had sunk, including 14 battleships. While all this was taking place a party of Stromness schoolchildren were enjoying an outing on the boat *Flying Kestrel*, and had a ringside seat of the great scuttle.

The British had been taken completely by surprise, and could do little more than watch the drama as it unfolded. Nine German sailors were killed during the scuttling, most of whom were shot by over-zealous British boarding parties as they tried to save some of the smaller German ships. Reuter and his men were duly shipped south to prison camps on the British mainland, and with that the last great drama of the war came to an end. In February the following year the Admiral Commanding Orkney and Shetland (ACOS) hauled down his flag, and Scapa Flow was deemed a secondary rather than a primary fleet base. Later that year it was redesignated as a minor naval anchorage, and the last warships departed.

During 1919 the coastal defence batteries were dismantled and the booms removed. For some reason the Admiralty was less willing to remove the blockships sunk in the eastern entrances to the Flow, which would re-open these small channels to fishing boats and commerce. In fact negotiations dragged on for more than a decade, and many of the blockships were still in place in 1939. The dangerous job of clearing minefields began in April 1919, and this Anglo-American operation continued for most of the year. During this time the US Naval minesweeping force was based in Kirkwall, and was responsible for clearing the 70,000 mines laid between Orkney and Southern Norway.

That still left the problem of the German High Seas Fleet. The seabed around the islands of Cava, Rysa and Fara were littered with the wrecks of German warships, some of which were still visible above the waves, and constituted a hazard to navigation. The Admiralty began half-hearted salvage attempts in 1919, raising the battleship *Baden* and a few smaller ships. In the early 1920s two small civilian contractors – one based in Stromness – began raising the odd destroyer, but it was not until 1924 that things began to happen in earnest. That year the Admiralty sold its rights to 26 destroyers and two battleships to the salvage firm of Cox & Danks. In 1926 they raised the destroyers, scuttled in Gutter Sound between Fara, Rysa Little and Hoy.

The following year they started work on the capital ships, raising the battlecruiser *Molke* using compressed air. More warships followed, including the battleship *Hindenburg*, raised in 1930, and the *Prinzregent Luitpold* in 1931. A collapse of the scrap metal market in the early 1930s led to Cox & Danks handing over their licences to another company, Metal Industries Ltd., who continued the operation on a more modest scale, raising a warship a

The great scuttle. After World War I the bulk of the German High Seas Fleet was interned in Scapa Flow. Then, on 21 June 1919 the Germans scuttled their own ships to prevent them being handed over to the British. In this photograph the battleship *Bayern* is seen sinking in the middle of the channel between Cava and Houton. (Author's collection)

year until 1939. The last vessel to be raised was the battlecruiser *Derfflinger*. Her upturned hull was still lying off Rysa when the war began, and she remained there for the duration of hostilities. Today the few remaining German warships provide scuba divers with one of the best wreck diving sites in the world.

By the 1920s Scapa Flow was completely defenceless, although it was still used as a fleet rendezvous during summer manoeuvres. The Atlantic Fleet visited Orkney almost every year from 1920 onwards, but there the preparations for another war ended. Sheep grazed amongst the derelict remains of the shore batteries, and even the local Territorial Army was no longer a force, as the Orcadian volunteer gunners had been disbanded in 1915, and their posts taken over by the Royal Marines. This created such bad feeling in the islands that the post-war Territorial Army found it almost impossible to find recruits until 1937, when the threat of another war encouraged the Orcadians to forgive the Army and rejoin the colours. The first local Territorial Army unit to be raised in 1937 was the 226th Heavy Anti-Aircraft Battery, which would see service in wartime Orkney. Other units followed, including the Orkney Heavy Regiment, Royal Artillery, which was trained in coastal defence.

As the threat of war grew, the Admiralty seemed to remember the potential offered by Scapa Flow. In April 1937 work began on the construction of oil tanks at Lyness, capable of holding a total of 100,000 tons of fuel oil for the fleet. The first of these tanks was operational by the start of 1938. In 1937 the sites of potential anti-submarine booms had been surveyed, and the booms were laid the following summer – in almost exactly the same places as the anti-submarine defences of World War I. The real increase in this defensive build-up took place after October 1937, when Scapa Flow was designated as a 'Category A' Defended Port. Unfortunately, it was defended by wind, location and tide, rather than by guns and mines.

Admiral Forbes, commanding the Home Fleet had reservations about the suitability of a near-defenceless Scapa Flow, and he encouraged the Admiralty to speed up its work. It was felt that the fleet could provide its own protection against enemy aircraft, but in the face of RAF estimates that the Luftwaffe could drop almost 450 tons of bombs on Scapa Flow in a day, it was clear that additional air defences were desperately needed. Two fighter squadrons were stationed at Wick on the Scottish mainland, and 24 heavy anti-aircraft guns were earmarked to augment the base defences. By January 1939, when the Admiralty declared that Scapa Flow would become its 'fleet base' in time of war, the actual defences in place were pitifully weak. At that time they consisted of the eight heavy AA guns operated by 226 Battery, stationed around Lyness, and four 6in. guns of World War I vintage, mounted as coastal defence pieces – two at the Ness Battery and two at Stanger Head. Another obsolete 4.7in. gun was ready to be put in place at the Neb Battery on Flotta. Men of the Orkney Heavy Regiment manned all of these guns.

However, things were improving. The Fleet Air Arm had already established a base, HMS *Sparrowhawk*, at Hatston, on the western outskirts of Kirkwall, the booms were in place across the entrances to Scapa Flow, and Admiral Forbes on board his flagship HMS *Nelson* established his floating headquarters on 'A-Buoy' off Flotta, which was equipped with phone lines to Lyness and a direct line to the War Cabinet in London. By August 1939 some 44 ships of the Home Fleet were based in Scapa Flow, including six battleships and battlecruisers, one aircraft carrier and Jellicoe's old flagship *Iron Duke*, which served as a headquarters ship.

During these last days of peace, the defences of Scapa Flow were in slightly better shape than they had been in 1914, but this time the technology of war meant that the threat posed by Germany was far greater than it had been. A new generation of U-boats had been produced, and for the first time Germany had the ability to attack Scapa Flow from the air. While the Admiralty and the War Cabinet had been slow to wake up to the threat posed by Germany, at least they knew more about the potential and the drawbacks of Scapa Flow than their counterparts had in the previous war. In the months which followed the outbreak of war the inadequate defences of Scapa Flow would be bolstered, in a race to make the base secure before the Germans could discover just how vulnerable the naval base really was.

PRINCIPLES OF DEFENCE: 'PLAN Q' AND 'PLAN R'

On 3 September 1939 Britain declared war on Germany, and once again Scapa Flow became Britain's main wartime naval base. That was when the War Office instituted 'Plan Q' – a blueprint for the wartime defence of Scapa Flow. It was a complex plan, calling for an integrated system of land, sea and air defence, and the creation of a base that was impenetrable to submarines, and well-enough defended to deter the Luftwaffe from even attempting to attack it. The anti-aircraft defences called for the emplacement of 80 heavy anti-aircraft (HAA) guns around the anchorage, supported by 40 light anti-aircraft (LAA) pieces. No fewer than 108 searchlights would be deployed, while 40 barrage balloons on land and on barges would deter low-level attacks directed at the main fleet anchorage.

First Lord of the Admiralty Winston Churchill actually disapproved of the plan, as he thought British resources should not be wasted on passive defence which tied down three AA regiments in Orkney for the duration of the war. However, he immediately approved the dispatch of an extra 16 3.7in. HAA guns, to augment the eight belonging to 266 Battery that were already sited where they could protect the Lyness fuel tanks. Twenty more were earmarked to be sent north before the end of the year. In mid-September Churchill journeyed to Scapa Flow to see the defences for himself, and visited HMS *Iron Duke*, the floating headquarters of Admiral Sir Wilfred French, Admiral Commanding Orkney and Shetland (ACOS).

In mid-September 1939 the army assumed control of the Orkney defences, and on 29 September Brigadier-General (later Major-General) Geoffrey Kemp MC arrived in Orkney to assume command of the Orkney and Shetland Defences (OSDef). Apparently he wanted to set up his headquarters in Kirkwall, but the most suitable building – The Kirkwall Hotel – was already occupied by Vice Admiral Max Horton and his staff. Horton was in charge of the Northern Patrol, which performed the same function as had its predecessors in the last war. Consequently Kemp decided to set up his headquarters in the Stromness Hotel instead.

When he arrived he was a commander with very little to command. The forces at his disposal consisted of the five coastal defence guns at the nearby Ness Battery and on Flotta, 226 Battery with its eight 4.5in. HAA guns at Lyness, and three Bren guns guarding the newly installed radar station at Netherbutton in the East Mainland. Finally he had a company of the 5th Battalion, Seaforth Highlanders, at his disposal, and a field company of Royal Engineers. His force of little over 500 men had to defend hundreds of kilometres of Orkney coastline, as well as protect the fleet in Scapa Flow. His staff consisted of a clerk with a typewriter, and a driver with a car. He even had to borrow a civilian boat in order to visit his naval counterpart on board the *Iron Duke*, or to inspect the batteries on Flotta.

His arrival coincided with the first German reconnaissance flights over Scapa Flow, which encouraged him to press the War Office for reinforcements. He also began work on a defensive plan – a scheme that would soon blossom into something akin to 'Plan Q' drawn up shortly before the war began. His first task was to establish the locations of the most important gun batteries and searchlight positions, and to coordinate anti-aircraft defence with Admiral French. The result was his first Operational Instruction, issued on 10 October, which permitted the engaging of any air targets under 1,200m (4,000ft) flying within ten kilometres (six miles) of the Home Fleet flagship mooring on 'A-Buoy'.

Within days Kemp received reinforcements – the rest of the 5th Battalion of Seaforths arrived, together with the 7th Battalion, Gordon Highlanders. He now commanded a brigade-sized force. The Gordons were ordered to take over the protection of vital points (VPs), which included the batteries on Flotta, the landward sides of the boom defences, as well as the telephone cable huts, wireless stations and radio masts that were sprouting around the Orkney landscape. Later that month two more field engineer companies arrived, which allowed Kemp to begin working on the construction of camps to house the labourers needed to put 'Plan Q' into effect.

Meanwhile the Admiralty were trying to play their part in improving Scapa Flow's defences. In 1938 blockships had been sunk to seal off the gaps in the eastern channels of Scapa Flow. The largest of these was Kirk Sound, between the Orkney Mainland at Holm and the small island of Lamb Holm. Although the channel was blocked by World War I blockships there were gaps that allowed small vessels to weave their way past the obstructions. While efforts had been made to seal these channels before the war began, they still remained vulnerable. Admiral Forbes inspected them in person in June 1939, and deemed them to be navigable, regardless of the claims made by the Admiralty. More blockships were purchased, and in September and early October 1939 these were sunk in position. The last channel to be sealed was Kirk Sound, and the 4,000-ton steamer SS *Lake Neuchâtel* was even in Scapa on the night of 14 October, waiting to be towed into place and scuttled.

That night *U-47*, commanded by Korvettenkapitän Günther Prien, passed through Kirk Sound, and penetrated the defences of Scapa Flow. Finding the main anchorage empty, Prien headed north, and spotted the battleship HMS *Royal Oak* lying beneath the cliffs of Gaitnip, a few kilometres from Scapa Pier. The U-boat fired a total of seven torpedoes at the battleship, hitting her with three of them. The *Royal Oak* sank in 13 minutes, taking 833 of her crew down with her. *U-47* then slipped out of Scapa Flow the way she had

The defences of Scapa Flow during World War II

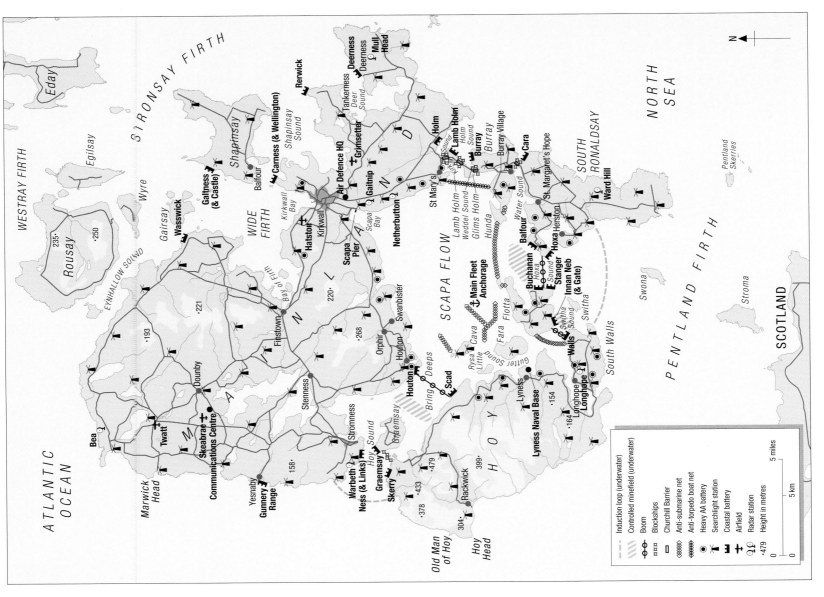

WESTRAY FIRTH

STRONSAY FIRTH

Eday

Egilsay

Wyre

Gairsay

Rousay
·235
·250

EYNHALLOW SOUND

Shapinsay

Balfour

Shapinsay Sound

NORTH SEA

Deerness
Deerness
Deerness
Mull Head

Rerwick

Carness (& Wellington)

Tankerness
Deer Sound

Gaitness (& Castle)

WIDE FIRTH

Kirkwall Bay

Grimsetter

Air Defence HQ

Gaitnip

Holm

Lamb Holm

Holm Sound

Burray
Burray Village

Cara

SOUTH RONALDSAY

Pentland Skerries

Kirkwall

Hatston

Scapa Pier

Scapa Bay

Netherbutton

St Mary's

Lamb Holm
Weddel Sound
Glims Holm
Hunda

St. Margaret's Hope

Ward Hill

Wasswick

Twatt

Bea

Skeabrae
Communications Centre

M A I N L A N D

·221

·193

Dounby

Finstown

·268

·220

Orphir

Swanbister

Houton

SCAPA FLOW

Main Fleet Anchorage

Water Sound

Balfour

Buchanan
Hoxa
Stanger
Inman Neb (& Gate)

Hoxa
Herston

Switha Sound
Switha

Walls

Stenness

Stromness

Graemsay
Hoy Sound

Warbeth
Ness (& Links)
Graemsay
Skerry

·158

Yesnaby
Gunnery Range

Rackwick

·479

·433

·378

·304

·399

Old Man of Hoy

Hoy Head

Marwick Head

ATLANTIC OCEAN

Houton

Scad

Bring Deeps

H O Y

Lyness

Lyness Naval Base

·154

·164

Longhope
Longhope

South Walls

Rysa Little
Cava
Fara
Flotta

Gutter Sound

Swona

Stroma

PENTLAND FIRTH

SCOTLAND

N

	Induction loop (underwater)
	Controlled minefield (underwater)
	Boom
	Blockships
	Churchill Barrier
	Anti-submarine net
	Anti-torpedo boat net
	Heavy AA battery
	Searchlight station
	Coastal battery
	Airfield
	Radar station
·479	Height in metres

0   5 miles

0   5 km

The crew of a Lewis gun, photographed on the perimeter of the Royal Naval Air Station HMS *Sparrowhawk*, possibly during an air attack on Scapa Flow in early 1940. By the summer of 1940 Orkney was bristling with light and heavy anti-aircraft weapons, and these proved sufficient to deter any further larger German attacks. (Orkney Library & Archives)

In this striking photograph a carrier platoon from an infantry battalion of the Orkney Garrison (probably the 7th Bn, Gordon Highlanders) conduct manoeuvres through the middle of the Ring of Brodgar, a circular 'henge' of Neolithic standing stones, surrounded by a wide ditch. (Private collection)

come in – weaving her way past the blockships of Kirk Sound. The *Lake Neuchâtel* was scuttled in Kirk Sound a week later, but by then the damage had already been done.

The *Royal Oak* disaster caused an uproar. The Admiralty were rightly blamed for leaving Scapa Flow so poorly defended, but somehow Churchill weathered the political storm. The commander of the Home Fleet, Admiral Sir Michael Forbes, declared that the anchorage was unsafe, a point which was reinforced three days after the disaster when Scapa Flow suffered its first air raid. He ordered the Home Fleet to disperse to other anchorages – the Firth of Forth and the Cromarty Firth on the North Sea coast of Scotland, and the Forth of Clyde and Loch Ewe on the west coast. Emergency meetings of the War Cabinet were held, while both the War Office and the Admiralty were forced to re-examine their plans. For his part Admiral Forbes remained convinced that Scapa Flow remained the best anchorage for the Home Fleet. All he asked was that it was properly protected.

The result was that an 'Inter-Services Committee for the Defence of the Fleet Anchorage of Scapa Flow' was hurriedly established in Whitehall, and a fairly lavish budget of £500,000 was approved for the construction of new defences, with more money available if it was needed. This time there would be no half measures. The result was 'Plan R'. This called for the implementation of 'Plan Q', augmented with a much more extensive network of coastal batteries, anti-submarine defences, radar stations, airfields, minefields and anti-invasion defences. As a result Orkney was going to become a fortress – the most heavily defended harbour in Europe.

By December 1939 construction contracts had been signed, guns allocated and anti-submarine nets ordered. Merchant ships arrived carrying construction materials, as well as everything from searchlights to barrage balloons. The garrison was heavily reinforced, and the new gun positions chosen by the newly

promoted Major-General Kemp were approved, and the foundations dug. Both the Fleet Air Arm and the Royal Air Force scoured Orkney for suitable sites for aerodromes, while anti-aircraft battery sites were chosen and the guns installed almost as soon as they could be unloaded. All this frenetic activity was taking place amid a particularly bad winter, where the gales, snow and rain seemed incessant.

Part of the reason for the haste was a deadline. As First Lord of the Admiralty Winston Churchill had forced the new Inter-Services Committee to declare that the Home Fleet would return to Scapa Flow on 1 March 1940. This was no arbitrary deadline. Instead it was based on the grim assessment that the dispersal of the fleet had weakened the ability of the Home Fleet to react to German naval movements. Intelligence suggested that the Germans might be planning a spring offensive, and Churchill wanted the fleet to be ready for action when the time came. This was the reason these construction workers dug foundations in the snow, or poured concrete in the teeth of a howling gale.

Fortunately the Luftwaffe left the garrison to its own devices, although the occasional reconnaissance and mine-laying flight continued throughout that first winter of the war. By February the first phase of coastal battery construction had been completed, and most of the booms and anti-submarine defences had been put in place. The biggest weakness lay in the anti-aircraft defence of the anchorage, as the only guns that were operational were those of 266 Battery at Lyness. A further 20 HAA guns were in their battery emplacements, and their crews were just assuming their duties. Kemp pushed his superiors and his men, and by the end of the month these guns were all operational, as were another 11 HAA guns and 13 light AA guns, supported by 28 of the 100 searchlights allocated to OSDef.

In the end Churchill's deadline was delayed by a week for operational reasons, by which time Kemp had increased his operational HAA complement to a healthy 52 guns. The targets set by 'Plan Q' were now well on their way to being met. On 8 March 1940 Churchill planned to enter Scapa Flow in style aboard HMS *Rodney*. However, a mine scare kept her at sea while the

A Bofors 40mm light anti-aircraft gun, deployed on 'The Citadel' outside Stromness, overlooking the Ness Battery (pictured on the right of the photograph) and Hoy Sound, the westerly entrance into Scapa Flow. (Private collection)

A German Junkers Ju 88 twin-engined bomber, photographed near the farm of Flotterston in Sandwick, on the West Mainland of Orkney. A Grumman Martlet from 804 Squadron of the Fleet Air Arm, based at RNAS Skeabrae, shot her down on Christmas Day 1940. (Private collection)

approaches to the anchorage were swept, so Churchill transferred to a destroyer, and made his entrance on board her. By that evening he was dining on board HMS *Hood*, which effectively sent the signal that Scapa Flow was safe, the fleet had returned and the Royal Navy was ready for action.

On his return to Whitehall Churchill reported to the War Cabinet that Scapa Flow was '80% secure', and the risk of attack on the fleet was acceptably low. It was during this visit that he approved the plan to build permanent anti-submarine barriers across the eastern channels leading into Scapa – the barriers which now bear his name. The deadline imposed by him, and the return of the fleet at that time, were both fortuitous. The first serious air raid on Scapa Flow was carried out by the Luftwaffe on the evening of 16 March, and increasingly heavy raids would follow in the weeks to come. Then, on 9 April, the Germans launched Operation *Weserübung* – their codename for the invasion of Denmark and Norway. The Home Fleet was ready and able to intervene, and consequently the German Navy (*Kriegsmarine*) suffered serious losses during

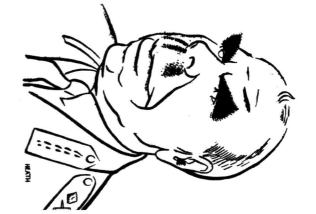

the operation, even though the German Army (Heer) managed so secure control of both countries, despite Allied intervention.

This meant that by the time the campaign ended in June 1940, the Kriegsmarine could use the Norwegian fjords as operational bases, while the Luftwaffe airfields in Norway were now within easy striking range of Scapa Flow. However, no such raids ever materialized, although reconnaissance and minelaying sorties continued throughout the war. This way largely owing to improvements in the anti-aircraft defences of Scapa Flow – by mid-April 1940 there were 88 HAA guns deployed around Scapa Flow, which more than fulfilled the requirements of 'Plan Q'. Major-General Kemp now commanded over 12,000 men, with two full brigades at his disposal. A hundred aircraft searchlights were in place, of which 88 were operational, and Orkney now boasted 14 coastal batteries, with most of the guns mounted in them ready for action.

More importantly, the fully integrated defensive system called for by 'Plan R' was now working, with these fixed defences capable of coordinating fire with the Royal Navy, while covering the complex network of booms, nets and mines that were now in place. The anti-aircraft defences of Orkney were provided with targeting information from several radar sites, which also helped fighter control direct their aircraft to intercept enemy planes. Of course there were setbacks – one day in April the RAF launched 40 barrage

Major-General Geoffrey C. Kemp, an artillery veteran of World War I and holder of the Military Cross, was the first commander of OSDef (Orkney & Shetland Defence Force), arriving to take command of the garrison in September 1939. (Private collection)

C DEFENCE OF THE ANCHORAGE: HOXA SOUND, 1940

During World War II the main entrance into Scapa Flow was extremely well defended, against all forms of attack. First, gun batteries on Hoxa Head (**1**) Stanger Head (**2**), Walls (**3**) and Innan Neb (**4**) with its associated secondary Neb and Gate Battery, all secured Hoxa Sound and Switha Sound from attack by enemy surface ships. Additional light batteries – the Buchan Battery on Hoxa Head (**5**) and the Balfour Battery on Flotta (see inset) provided additional protection against E-boats or other fast attack craft. A control position on Stanger Head (see inset) provided a vantage point from which the defence of the entrance could be coordinated.

Searchlight and anti-aircraft positions dotted the area, while barrage balloons helped protect the main fleet anchorage from attack by low-flying enemy aircraft. Underwater protection was provided by a magnetic induction loop (thick red line), and by controlled minefields (red slashes), and by anti-torpedo nets, which were also strung from barges in the main anchorage. Finally anti-shipping booms blocked Hoxa Sound and Switha Sound.

C Defence of the anchorage: Hoxa Sound, 1940

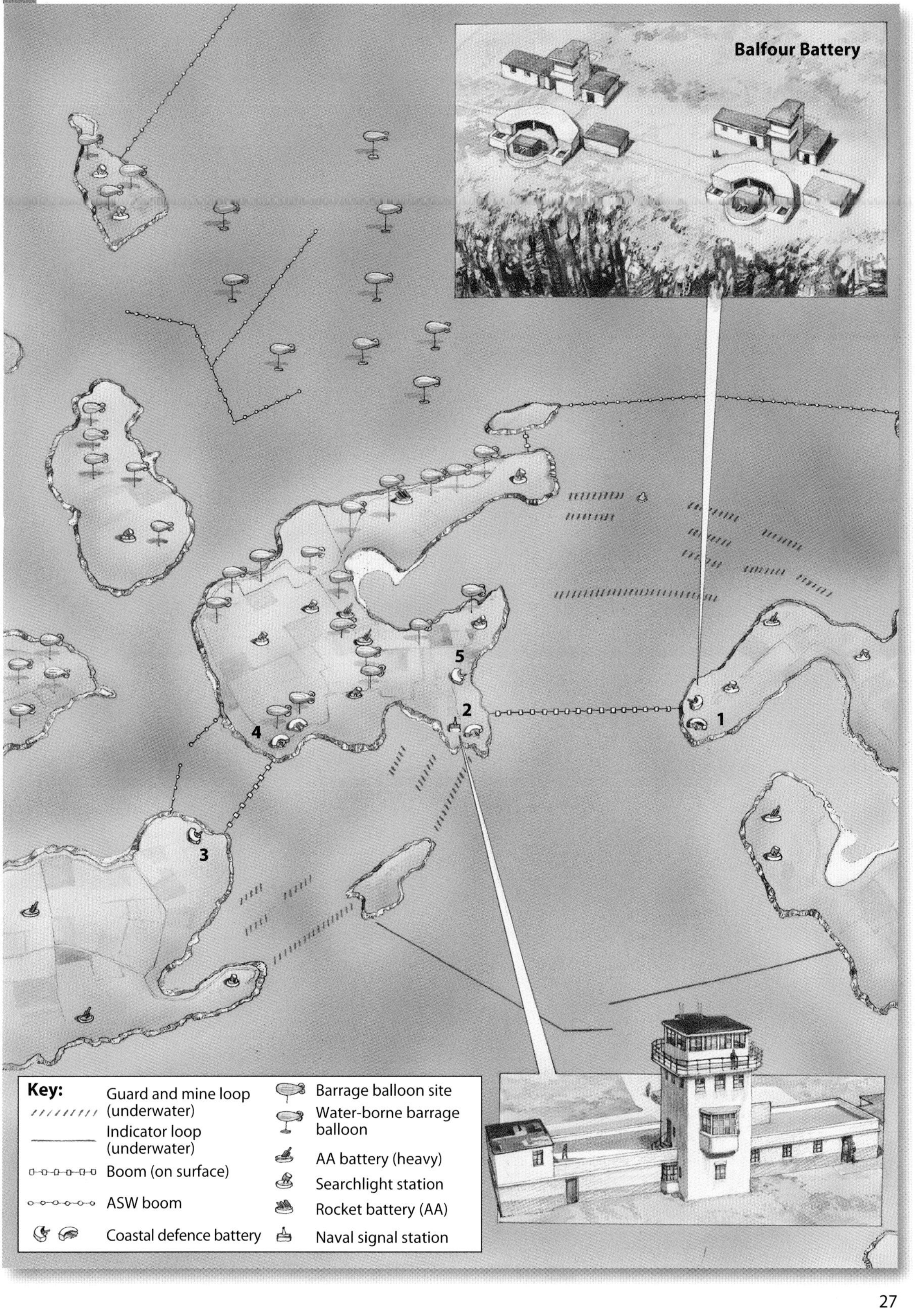

Balfour Battery

1

2

3

4

5

Key:

///// Guard and mine loop (underwater)	Barrage balloon site
—— Indicator loop (underwater)	Water-borne barrage balloon
▫-▫-▫-▫ Boom (on surface)	AA battery (heavy)
◦-◦-◦-◦ ASW boom	Searchlight station
Coastal defence battery	Rocket battery (AA)
	Naval signal station

Major-General Slater took over command of OSDef in January 1943, and remained in charge of the Orkney Garrison until the last months of the war, when OSDef was downgraded to a brigade-sized rather than a divisional command. (Private collection)

balloons around the anchorage – the full quantity specified in the two plans. A sudden gale then came from nowhere, and all but one of them were ripped from their tethers and lost. However, it was clear that by the summer of 1940 the defences of Scapa Flow were formidable. The Germans were well aware of their scale, which explains why they never attempted another attack against the anchorage, despite the proximity of their Norwegian bases. Orkney was now an impregnable fortress.

A TOUR OF THE FORTRESS

The easiest way to take a look at how the defences of Scapa Flow worked as an integrated system of defence is to take a virtual snapshot of these defences, as they looked in the summer of 1940. While each played a part in supporting the other elements, the Orkney Garrison worked together with the Home Fleet to ensure there were no chinks in these defences. However, for clarity it might be easier if we break this island fortress down into its major component parts.

Radar and anti-aircraft defences

One of the real advantages of Orkney as a base was that it was a group of islands, which, at least in theory, meant that it was extremely difficult for incoming aircraft to avoid being detected on radar. Shortly before the war began a primitive and pioneering 'Chain Home' radar device was shipped north from Yorkshire, and installed at Netherbutton, a site on the East Mainland that overlooked Scapa Flow, midway between Kirkwall and the village of St Mary's. While this probably wasn't the best location to detect inbound low-level aircraft approaching Scapa Flow from the west, the land to the east of the radar station was reasonably flat, and it was discovered that aircraft flying over 1,200m (4,000ft) could be detected – if the set worked properly.

Even more haphazard than the radar coverage was the way this information was passed to the fleet and the garrison. A direct phone line was established between Admiral French on board HMS *Iron Duke*, and an RAF corporal in Netherbutton. The Admiral was the only man in the garrison who could issue air-raid warnings, something he did after consulting with the corporal. The warning was then passed around the fleet, and to the gunners of 266 HAA Battery at Lyness.

By early 1940 the situation had improved dramatically. In April the Luftwaffe launched several raids on Scapa Flow, and by then the primitive set at Netherbutton had been replaced by a more reliable 'Chain Home Low' set, while the 'Ceres Class' anti-aircraft cruiser HMS *Curlew* anchored in Scapa Flow augmented this radar coverage with its own set, an even more reliable Type 79B radar, which had an effective range of anything up to 145km (90 miles), compared with the 40km (25 miles) range of the Netherbutton apparatus. An Army gunnery officer on board passed on targeting information to all of the Army's anti-aircraft batteries, while his naval counterpart did the same around the fleet.

By the end of 1940 many HAA batteries were equipped with gun-layer (GL) radars, and it was discovered that these could detect and direct fire against aircraft flying as low as 150m (500ft). In fact, as these battery radars became operational the need for searchlights decreased, as the radar-directed anti-aircraft guns could engage targets by day or night. Later in the war additional radar stations were established at South Walls in Hoy, at Start

Point in Sanday, on the north-east coast of the Orkney Mainland at Birsay and on Ward Hill in South Ronaldsay. This provided all-round radar coverage, and these sets had the capability to detect low-lying aircraft and surface targets as well as high-flying enemy bombers.

The HAA batteries themselves usually consisted of up to eight guns apiece, with communications links to searchlight positions and to a central command post. Still, during the German raid in March 1940 this arrangement was less effective than had been hoped, prompting Kemp and Admiral Binney (the new ACOS) to develop a new system. Known as the 'Scapa Barrage', this aimed to put up a curtain of flak in the path of oncoming aircraft, the gun positions firing on a fixed angle and bearing set by the general officer commanding (GOC). The warships of the Home Fleet were invited to add their weight to the barrage, and a trial 'shoot' was arranged on 26 March. It was a great success, forming 'a complete curtain'. The system was approved, and was used with great effectiveness during the Luftwaffe raids of 1940.

Finally, low-level protection to the fleet was afforded by LAA guns such as Bren, Lewis and Vickers guns covering key points, while the network of 80 barrage balloons were designed to keep German aircraft from conducting torpedo attacks on the warships in the main anchorage. Another novel scheme was the 'Z' rocket battery located on Roan Head in Flotta. A total of 164 rockets would be fired in a mass barrage at enemy aircraft, and while nobody expected them to be particularly effective, they would certainly distract the enemy pilots and bomb aimers. An even less successful scheme was the use of smoke generators to obscure targets. The Orkney winds rendered this system highly ineffective. By the summer of 1940 the air defences of Orkney were considered more than adequate to deter even the largest German raid, thereby providing the Home Fleet with the safe haven it so desperately needed.

A Type 277S Search Radar, one of two mounted in the ancillary radar station on Ward Hill, South Ronaldsay, in 1944. While it could detect aircraft at a range of 40km (25 miles), its primary function was as a surface search radar. (Stratford Archive)

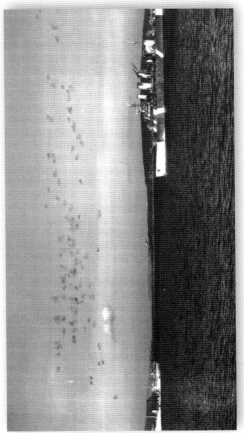

One of the principal roles of the Orkney garrison was to provide anti-aircraft protection for the fleet. One tactic at its disposal was the 'Scapa Barrage', a curtain of flak designed to deter enemy aircraft from approaching the anchorage. In this photograph of the barrage in action the heavy cruiser HMS *Berwick* is pictured at anchor off Flotta. (Private collection)

Naval anti-aircraft gunners engage in target practice at the Northern Range, a gunnery centre at Yesnaby on the West Mainland. Aircraft would tow targets past the cliff-top battery, allowing sailors to hone their skills using live ammunition. (Stratford Archive)

An isolated searchlight position on the shore in front of the Houton Battery, overlooking the Bring Deeps, where the Hoy Sound entered Scapa Flow. The 36in. searchlight mounted in the building was powered by cables running from the battery engine room located at the top of the cliff and further up the steep hill leading to the battery itself. (Author's collection)

Coastal defences

By the summer of 1940 there were no fewer than 19 coastal batteries covering the approaches to Scapa Flow and Kirkwall Bay and, by 1943, this total had increased to 25. Of these, many were built on the sites of the coastal defence positions of the last war, although improvements in gun technology and changes in the way that gunfire was directed meant that these newer defences were far more effective than their predecessors.

Two batteries now covered the entrance to Hoy Sound – Ness Battery (two × 6in. BL guns) and the nearby Links Battery (two × 12-pdrs QF, replaced by one × twin 6-pdr QF in October 1940). By July the Skerry Battery on Hoy became operational (two × twin 6-pdrs QF), while in 1943 another small-calibre position – the Graemsay Battery (one × twin 6-pdr QF) augmented the 'anti motor torpedo boat' (AMTB) armament of the other batteries. On the other end of Hoy Sound at the Bring Deeps, the Houton Battery (two × 12-pdrs QF)

The Holm Battery overlooking Kirk Sound and Holm Sound is one of the better preserved coastal batteries in Orkney. It was commissioned in 1940 and remained in use until late 1943, when work on the Churchill Barriers made these defences unnecessary. (Author's collection)

on the Mainland in Orphir and Scad Head on Hoy (two × 12-pdrs QF, replaced in 1941 by one × twin 6-pdr QF) covered both ends of the Houton Boom.

The approaches to Hoxa Sound were protected by the Hoxa Battery on Hoxa Head (two × 6in. BL guns) and the Stanger Battery on Stanger Head (two × 6in. BL guns), while the Hoxa Boom was swept by the Buchanan Battery in Flotta (two × 12-pdrs QF, replaced by one × twin 6-pdr QF in January 1941) and the Balfour Battery on South Ronaldsay, close to the Hoxa Battery position (two × 12-pdrs QF, replaced by two × twin 6-pdrs QF in March 1941). Nearby Switha Sound was protected by the solitary gun of the Innan Neb Battery on Flotta (1 × 4.7in. QF), and the nearby Gate Battery (two × 12-pdrs QF). In 1941 the Neb Battery was installed in the midst of the Gate Battery (1 × twin 6-pdr. QF). By late 1943 another position – the Walls Battery (one × twin 6-pdr QF) on South Walls became operational.

Four batteries covered the small channels on the eastern side of Scapa Flow. The Holm Battery (two × 12-pdrs QF, augmented by a twin 6-pdr QF in September 1940) covered Holm Sound and Kirk Sound, while the Lamb Holm Battery on the island of the same name (two × 12-pdrs QF) swept the south side of Holm Sound and the approaches to Weddel Sound. On Burray the Burray Battery (two × 12-pdrs QF, replaced in February 1941 by one × twin 6-pdr QF) covered Weddel Sound, while the Cara Battery (two × 12-pdrs QF) on the northern tip of South Ronaldsay swept Water Sound. The building

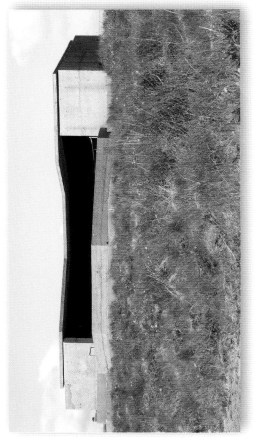

One of the two 6in. Mark VII gun emplacements which constituted the Ness Battery near Stromness. The battery was built in 1938, and during World War II its guns were manned by gunners of the 534th Coast Regiment. (Author's collection)

The battery observation post (BOP) of the Hoxa Head Battery. From this building the fire of the battery's two 6in. guns could be directed at targets approaching Hoxa Sound from the Pentland Firth. (Author's collection)

of the Churchill Barriers rendered these four coastal batteries obsolete, so during 1943–44 they were abandoned, and placed in care and maintenance (C&M).

That left the six batteries covering the northern side of Orkney, and the approaches to Kirkwall Bay. They were also there to deter any ships held in the contraband inspection anchorage in Kirkwall Bay from trying to escape. The most easterly of these was the Rerwick Battery, on Rerwick Head in Tankerness (two × 4.7in. QFs, replaced by two × 6in. BL guns from HMS *Iron Duke* in April 1941), which covered the approaches to Shapinsay Sound, while further to the west the Wellington Battery (three × 6in. BL guns from HMS *Iron Duke*) at Carness sealed off the entrance to Kirkwall Bay. Although this battery wasn't operational at the time of our chosen 'snapshot' of the defences (June 1940), it was fully operational two months later. In March 1941 it was

expanded to include the Carness Battery (two × 12-pdrs QF), whose emplacements were built a few metres to the east of the larger guns.

That left the northern approaches to Kirkwall Bay, between the Orkney Mainland in Evie and the island of Shapinsay. Two small batteries were built to cover this stretch of water, known as the Wide Firth. The Wasswick Battery on the Orkney Mainland in Evie (two × 12-pdrs QF) covered Gairsay Sound and the eastern approaches to the Wide Firth, while five kilometres to the east on Shapinsay the Galtness Battery, on the north-western side of Shapinsay (one × 12-pdr QF, replaced in March 1941 by one × twin 6-pdr QF), covered the western entrance to the Wide Firth. Two other small batteries would follow later in the war. In May 1941 the small Deerness Battery was completed (one × 12-pdr QF) to cover the anti-invasion boom stretched across the mouth of Deer Sound, and in September 1941 the Castle Battery (two × 4.7in. QF) entered service on Shapinsay, sited close to the existing Galtness Battery. Its purpose was to strengthen the defences of the Contraband Inspection Anchorage.

The construction of all these batteries represented a monumental achievement, particularly as the guns and much of the raw material had to be transported to Orkney, and then unloaded on what were often very inaccessible and remote locations. For command and logistical purposes the coastal batteries were grouped into three 'coast regiments': 533 (Southern) Defence Regiment based in Flotta, 534 (Western) Defence Regiment based in Stromness and 535 (Eastern) Defence Regiment based in Kirkwall.

Anti-invasion defences

One of the first tasks of the commander of OsDeF was to deal with the threat of enemy landings. This was seen as a fairly remote possibility until the German invasion of Norway, but after that the threat was a very real one. While this might not have taken the form of a full-scale amphibious invasion, there was a strong possibility that small commando-style raiding parties might be landed under cover of darkness, charged with damaging key defences. The other great fear was of a large-scale parachute landing, a tactic the Germans had used effectively elsewhere in Europe.

OSDef Operation Order 2 issued in October 1939 reported that Inganess Bay to the east of Kirkwall was a likely landing spot, as was Dingieshowe on the East Mainland. Pillboxes and beach defences were built to cover both beaches. Likely places for parachute and glider landing sites were in the relatively flat East Mainland, the north of the West Mainland, or in the southern portion of Hoy. Consequently the Army and Royal Marines created defensive positions on the Hill of Heddle near Finstown in the middle of the Orkney Mainland and at Wee Fea Hill overlooking Lyness in Hoy. Defensive perimeters were also established around the Netherbutton Radar Station, Lyness Naval Base and several important coastal batteries, including Stanger Head, Hoxa Head, Carness, Rerwick Head and the Ness Battery.

Mobile reserves were stationed in the parish of Holm in the south side of the East Mainland and in Stromness. By the summer of 1940 these static

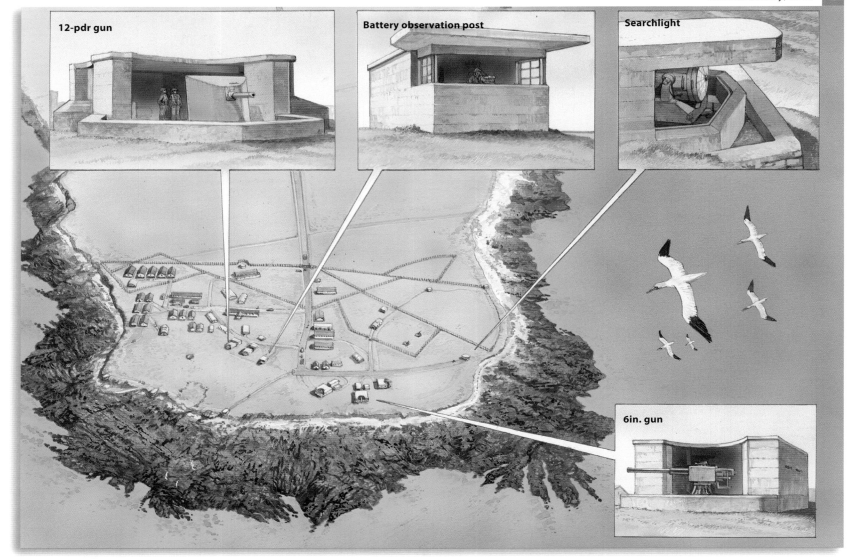

12-pdr gun

Battery observation post

Searchlight

6in. gun

D **CARNESS BATTERY, 1941**

Although it was one of the larger gun batteries in Orkney, Carness was typical of the gun positions which protected the islands during World War II. Technically Carness consisted of two batteries, as the three 6in. guns formed the Wellington Battery, whose guns (see inset) were taken from HMS *Iron Duke*.

Two 12-pdr Quick Firing (QF) guns were added in March 1941, to provide protection against fast attack boats. These weapons were housed in small emplacements (inset), and their fire was directed from an adjacent battery observation post (inset). Finally a string of four positions just behind the foreshore contained powerful 36in. searchlights. The battery complex and its attendant camp were protected from attack by barbed wire and pillboxes.

beach defences had been expanded to include other sites – the bays of Berstane and Meil to the east of Kirkwall were mined, while more barbed wire and pillboxes covered the exits from several other beaches, particularly around Dingieshowe, Inganess Bay, Deer Sound and Newark Bay on the East Mainland. Anti-tank 'dragon's teeth' were sown in several beaches, supported by steel girder obstacles, while trenches and machine-gun positions were dug into the ground overlooking these beaches. Company-sized garrisons were posted around Orkney, where they could react even more effectively to any threat. By June 1940 these defences were formidable, particularly as any invasion force or raiding party would have to reach Orkney through seas covered by patrolling warships and aircraft, and swept by radar.

Anti-submarine and anti-surface ship defences

Of all the aspects of Scapa Flow's defences, with one notable exception, these were almost exact copies of the defences put in place around Scapa Flow during World War I. The first elements to be put in place were the anti-shipping booms and the anti-submarine boom nets. Work began in June

These stylish director towers (DTs) of the Balfour Battery were built immediately behind the battery's two twin 6-pdr gun emplacements. These guns were primarily designed to be used against enemy E-boats or destroyers attempting to ram the Hoxa Boom. (Author's collection)

1938, supervised by the boom defence officer, Scapa, based in Rysa Lodge in Hoy. He was hindered by having only two boom vessels and one netlayer at his disposal, but by the end of the year the Hoxa booms (both anti-shipping and anti-submarine versions) were in place. The system worked – that September the battleship HMS *Resolution* steamed into the anti-shipping boom, and it not only held, but brought the battleship to a halt.

By the outbreak of war the Switha and Houton booms were also in place, although the Admiralty requested that the anti-shipping booms be strengthened

by doubling them up with two lines of floats rather than just one. This reinforcing work would still not be completed by the summer of 1940. HMS *Pomona*, the Boom Defence Command established at Lyness, was responsible for maintaining these nets and booms, leaving the Scapa boom defence to operate the growing fleet of boom defence vessels and converted trawlers that actually opened and closed the booms, and patrolled them throughout the war. An additional light anti-shipping boom was erected between the Orkney Mainland in Holm and the north-western corner of Burray, although the decision to add this boom came after these eastern defences had been penetrated by *U-47* in October 1939.

Similarly, the business of sealing these small eastern channels with blockships was still under way when the war began, and Kirk Sound was still navigable when the *U-47* made her attack. As a result the number of blockships was increased and, in May 1940, Churchill approved the construction of permanent barriers across these small channels, with work beginning on the 'Churchill Barriers' later that year.

During World War I the system of induction loops to provide early warning of approaching U-boats and the smaller guard loops and controlled minefields worked very well, and so the decision was made in late 1939 to lay a similar system across Hoxa Sound, Switha Sound and Hoy Sound. The minefields were laid in early 1940, as part of 'Plan R', and additional minefields were added in 1941. The indicator loops were in place by the summer of 1940, but they proved to be prone to malfunction, particularly the one sited in the approaches to Hoy Sound, which was exposed to damage from the strong tides. Both sets of loops had to be replaced after each winter, owing to seabed damage. The less exposed guard loops were less problematic, although the controlled minefields had to be replaced frequently in case the mines became defective and exploded of their own accord. That meant they had to be destroyed before being replaced – a spectacle which was regarded as a 'definite advantage to morale'.

In World War I hydrophone listening stations had been established in the main channels, but in World War II these had been replaced by slightly more sophisticated harbour defence asdic (HDA). This was used off Flotta in early

The battered remains of anti-ship boom defences lying on the Burray shoreline next to Barrier No. 3. These would originally have formed part of the boom stretched across either Hoxa Sound, Hoy Sound or Switha Sound. (Author's collection)

1940 and proved reasonably effective. Still, when the HDA network was extended out to sea in 1942 and again in 1945, it proved less reliable and was particularly prone to detecting passing fish and tidal swirls rather than man-made contacts.

Finally there were the defences set around the main anchorage itself. First, a string of anti-submarine booms were erected to the north of Flotta and off Cava, in an attempt to prevent U-boats from crossing from one side of the anchorage to the other. A more unusual form of defence was provided from 1942 onwards by a screen of landing craft tanks (LCTs) fitted with anti-torpedo baffles designed to protect the warships from torpedoes. They proved difficult to keep in position in bad weather, and were something of a hazard to shipping. When they were withdrawn in early 1944 amid the D-Day preparations, their departure was generally viewed with relief.

Air cover

In 1938 the Air Ministry conducted a survey in Orkney looking for suitable sites to build airfields. In September of the same year the Admiralty conducted its own survey and selected Skeabrae in the West Mainland and Hatston outside Kirkwall as locations for naval air stations. The Hatston site was purchased early 1939 and work began immediately. Unusually the airfield had tarmac runways, making it the first non-grass airfield in Britain. The

E | ## THE BUILDING OF THE CHURCHILL BARRIERS

When *U-47* penetrated the defences of Scapa Flow in October 1939 it sailed through Holm Sound, one of the four small eastern entrances into Scapa Flow. While additional blockships were sunk to prevent another such raid, it was clear that a better form of defence was required. The solution was the construction of the Churchill Barriers – one of the most ambitious engineering projects of the war.

Four barriers were required, to span the four channels between the Orkney Mainland and the islands of Lamb Holm,

Glims Holm, Burray and South Ronaldsay. The construction method was deceptively simple. First a strip of stone rubble was laid along the length of the channel (**1**). When this broke the surface the rubble causeway was flanked by concrete blocks (**2**), and then the whole structure was flanked by a jumble of even larger blocks (**3**), to protect the structure from wave erosion. Finally the surface of the causeway was surmounted by a road (**4**), which turned the Churchill Barriers from a purely military undertaking into a civil project.

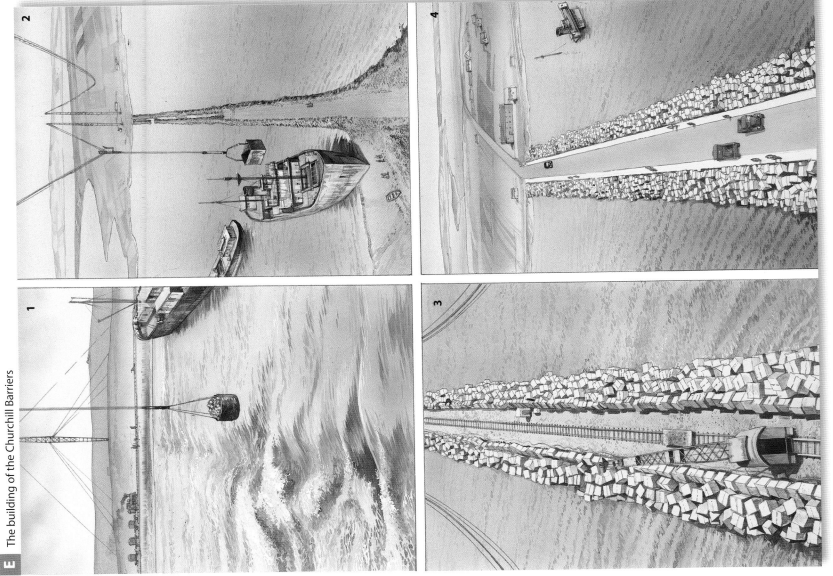

Swordfish torpedo bombers of 819 Squadron, Fleet Air Arm, being prepared for a practice sortie. The photograph was taken in March 1942 at HMS *Sparrowhawk*, the naval air station at Hatston outside Kirkwall. (Private collection)

airfield – dubbed HMS *Sparrowhawk* – was operational by the time the war began in September. At first it was a fully operational airfield, flying anti-submarine patrols and anti-shipping strikes in Norwegian waters. In April 1940 Sea Skuas flying from Hatston attacked and sank the German cruiser *Königsberg* off the Norwegian port of Bergen. However, by December 1940 it had become a training and support base for the carrier aircraft and seaplanes from the fleet, and during the war some 72 squadrons would use it as a temporary base.

The airfield in Wick, where three RAF squadrons were based – two of which were equipped with Hurricanes – provided fighter cover for Orkney. By November 1939 the decision was made to bolster this by the construction of three new airfields in Orkney, the result of which was the construction of the airfields at Twatt and Skeabrae in the West Mainland, and Grimsetter airfield at the head of Inganess Bay in the East Mainland, just outside Kirkwall. The RAF operated from Grimsetter and took over control of Skeabrae, while the Fleet Air Arm retained control of Twatt, just three kilometres to the north, which became known as HMS *Tern*. In 1943 Grimsetter was handed over to the Navy, becoming HMS *Robin*.

The three fighter squadrons based in Castletown and Wick in Caithness on the Scottish mainland provided excellent air cover for the Orkney defences, intercepting enemy reconnaissance aircraft far out over the North Sea. The first patrols were flown from RAF Skeabrae in September 1940, while its satellite RAF Grimsetter entered operational service the following month. The last of the airfields, HMS *Tern* (Twatt) became operational in June 1941. To confuse the Germans five dummy airfields were created during early 1940 – two at Birsay in the West Mainland, and one each on the islands of Rousay, Shapinsay and Sanday. Once the airfields in Orkney became operational these were integrated into an air-defence system, controlled at first by Coastal Command based at Wick, and later from the fighter control centre outside Kirkwall. By 1943 a fighter director school was established at Twatt, and for the rest of the war the Orkney airfields provided an excellent training facility for RAF and Fleet Air Arm pilots, radar directors and ground controllers alike.

The control tower at Twatt Airfield, one of four major airfields built in Orkney during World War II. Twatt and Grimsetter served the needs of the RAF, while Skeabrae and Hatston were operated by the Fleet Air Arm. (Author's collection)

The Home Fleet

The final element in the Scapa Flow defences was the Royal Navy itself. Naturally the bulk of the Home Fleet could not be employed on static defences, but while the warships were in Scapa Flow they were expected to add their weight to the 'Scapa barrage'. Even before that, warships were detailed off as temporary anti-aircraft batteries – HMS *Royal Oak* had been performing exactly this function as the AA defence for Kirkwall when she was torpedoed and sunk in October 1939. Other warships served longer spells as guard ships, radar pickets and command ships.

Of course the Royal Navy was heavily involved in the defence of the anchorage in other ways. The fleet of boom defense vessels, drifter and other small craft protected the entrances to Scapa Flow, while destroyers and cruisers maintained constant patrols off the entrances to the anchorage, in

A Royal Navy Walrus seaplane coming ashore on the jetty at Hatston, just outside Kirkwall. One of the functions of the naval air station there was to service the spotting aircraft of the Home Fleet. During the war Kirkwall Bay was used as a contraband control harbour, so many of the merchant vessels in the background were probably neutral vessels, awaiting inspection by the Royal Navy. (Private collection)

Known locally as 'The Black Building' after the pitch-based waterproof coating which once covered the structure, this building on the eastern edge of Kirkwall served as the main fighter direction station. (Author's collection)

the Pentland Firth, and in the North Sea approaches to Orkney. The waters surrounding the islands were regularly swept for mines, while escorts were provided for convoys passing through the Pentland Firth.

Then there was the Northern Patrol, which enforced the naval blockade of Nazi-occupied Europe by sealing the waters between Britain and Iceland to enemy or neutral shipping. Suspected neutrals were brought into Kirkwall Bay, where the ships and cargoes were inspected. This thankless but important job continued throughout the war, much as it had done in the previous conflict.

The Lyness Naval Base expanded rapidly during 1940. When HMS *Iron Duke* was damaged in September 1939 the base headquarters (and the flag of ACOS) was moved to Lyness, and renamed HMS *Proserpine*. It soon developed into a major command and communication centre, particularly after a new communications building was constructed on Wee Fea Hill, overlooking the Lyness base. Wee Fea was operational by 1943, and handled over 8,000 calls and signals a day, providing a link between ACOS, the ships of the fleet, other shore bases, and the Admiralty.

The above-ground oil tanks at Lyness were operational when the war began, and additional underground tanks were constructed during the conflict. The base harbour was expanded, including a 183m waterfront dubbed 'Golden Wharf' because of the high cost of its construction. Lyness served both as a headquarters, a refuelling and repair base, a boom defence workshop, a place of recreation and a home to thousands of servicemen. This made it the true hub of the anchorage. By the summer of 1940 the fleet anchorage was fully laid out, with an anchorage area for larger ships laid out to the north of Flotta (just where it was during the previous war), and a secondary anchorage for destroyers and other smaller ships on the opposite side of Flotta, closer to Lyness.

Above all, the Home Fleet needed the safety and security afforded by the defences of Scapa Flow. It was from here that its ships sailed to attack the Germans in the waters off Norway, gave chase to German surface units that managed to break out into the Atlantic, and escorted the vital convoys which crossed the North Atlantic, or sailed through the bitterly contested waters of the Arctic. It was vital that these ships and their crews were able to feel safe in Scapa Flow, where they could enjoy a temporary respite from the dangers facing them on the high seas. The ability of Scapa Flow's defences to offer this security was its greatest wartime achievement.

LIFE IN THE ORKNEY GARRISON

What then of the thousands of servicemen, soldiers, sailors, airmen and marines who garrisoned Orkney during the two world wars? What about the Orcadians themselves, forced to live and work inside a huge armed camp? Fortunately the 20th century was a time of mass literacy and hundreds of servicemen and some servicewomen wrote of their experiences, reflecting the loathing they felt for their remote posting and its climate, the boredom they suffered from and the everyday routines that dominated several years of their young lives.

In the early days of World War I, Admiral Jellicoe was so concerned at the lack of defences in Scapa Flow that he kept the Grand Fleet at sea most of the time, only returning to Scapa to refuel. Even when *U-18* was rammed and forced to beach off Orkney on 23 November 1914, communication problems meant the Navy was slow to react. When an Orcadian Territorial gunner telephoned the naval headquarters in Longhope to report the spotting of the beached U-boat, he was brusquely asked whether he knew the difference between a U-boat and a whale. The gunner replied that if it was a whale, then it had 25 men on its back.

While conditions were harsh for the sailors, whose ships spent much of their time at sea, it was far worse for the men building the emplacements, or manning them through the winter. One of these soldiers wrote about his experience:

As a Corporal of Royal Marines I was sent, along with two other privates, to the signal station on the island of Flotta. We landed on Flotta in appalling weather on 1st January 1915. At that time the only place for us was a mud hut, with planks across the top, covered by turf to keep out the rain. In the hut was a box with all the flags and pennants jumbled up, three berths, a telephone and a cracked combustion stove. This stove had to be used for all heating and cooking. The fuel used was peat. For the first few months we had to even sleep with all our clothes on (plus great coats) in an effort to keep warm. The turf did not keep out very much of the rain and so in addition to being cold, we were wet through for most of the time.

While conditions for the garrison improved with time, conditions were still harsh and the 'top brass' were often less than understanding. For instance, one camp was only issued with stoves to warm its huts after three years of waiting. Still, it was probably better than being on the Western Front, although conditions in winter were often so bad that servicemen regularly volunteered for the trenches rather than face another winter in Orkney. Almost as bad for morale as the climate was the boredom. While

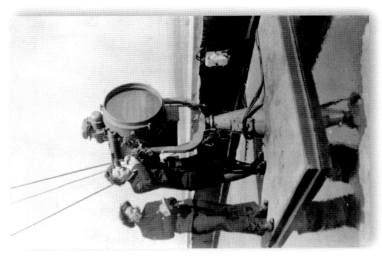

Wrens operating a 20in. signal projector outside the communications centre at Wee Fea, above Lyness Naval Base. During World War II women of the WRNS formed an integral part of the Orkney garrison, serving as communications, supply, repair and administration staff. (Orkney Library & Archives)

Sport provided a relief from the boredom of service life in Orkney, and most warships, batteries, airfields and shore facilities fielded their own teams that competed against each other. This was one of the more unusual sides in Orkney, as it was composed of Italian prisoners of war, from the Lamb Holm POW Camp. (Orkney Library & Archives)

training, inspections and the routine of garrison life helped fill the void, for many men on the ships and those guarding them the war seemed interminable.

When World War II began, the same lack of organization and miserable conditions were repeated. At first, most of the garrison was Orcadians, so at least they were used to the autumnal Orkney climate. The problems arrived when the reinforcements did. Billy Tait, a former Orkney gunner recalled how the Orkney Territorials set to digging roads to their battery positions in Flotta, building huts and latrines, and generally improving their camp. Senior officers from regular British regiments were horrified that Orkney Territorial officers were working alongside their men. However, others praised the ability of the Orcadians to work so well without supervision.

A gunner from an AA regiment posted to Orkney in winter found the place utterly miserable:

Our main and strongest emotion, I'm sure, was frustration at our enforced inactivity in that remote backwater at a time when most of our comrades of the AA Command were firing themselves shell-happy in the blitz. Believe me, we envied them! Mud, cold darkness and wind formed the general background. We found our way about the site on a precarious network of duckboards. The cold was such that there were times when I couldn't understand how water could feel so cold and yet remain unfrozen. It never really got light at all, and the gloom of midday was more depressing than the night itself.

Another recalled, 'Scapa! I was there in 1939 when the "amenities" were mostly claptrap huts floating in a sea of mud. Shocking conditions. The wet canteen [bar] was a large hut, a trestle table, and two or three large beer barrels. Imagine Klondike in the earliest days, and you have it.' Of course, camps on the Mainland, or near Lyness in Hoy had access to cinemas, shops, pubs and the other basic recreational facilities. Gunners on Hoxa Head or Stanger Head must have envied these colleagues.

Of course, with so many servicemen, the Wrens, WAAF and other female members of the garrisons found themselves in high demand. One Wren

remembered that; 'At the WRNS Training Department, a member of my course was drafted to the Orkneys. I hastened to commiserate with her. "What are you worried about?" She said. "There are six hundred men to every girl, and I'm going to enjoy myself."'

There were other advantages. Orkney was (and still is) a prosperous farming community, and food that was rationed or impossible to find in the south was regular fare in Orkney – bacon and eggs were regularly served at breakfast. Of course, there were those who never saw past the boredom and the climate. One RAF airman manning a barrage balloon site on Flotta said after the war 'The island was ringed by barrage balloons, and when these were up it appeared to be suspended in the water. How I wished they could cut the ropes and let the whole lot sink!' Another airman on his way to Orkney meeting a sailor on the ferry crossing, who was even more despondent:

I sat on deck somewhere near the prow of the ship, and a sailor returning from leave sat next to me. He hated the Orkneys; he hated that bloody Scapa Flow which was the reason for his being there, he'd rather be anywhere than in the bloody Orkneys; he was going to see his CO and ask for a Middle East posting; he'd rather go without leave than be up here. Life up here was too bloody lonely, too bloody meagre, too bloody cold! He broke down and cried. Nonplussed, amazed and innocent, I offered him my only bar of chocolate.

The servicemen even had a name for this malaise. They called it 'Orkneyitis'. While it probably existed in World War I nobody put a name to it. The symptoms were depression and erratic behaviour caused by boredom, monotony, isolation, the weather, the long winter nights and a lack of stimulation. Some gunners kept imaginary pets, sailors tended imaginary gardens on board ship and mild eccentricity was commonplace. The worst cases were found in remote camps, such as searchlight positions or AA batteries far from the rest of the garrison. One AA gunner said of his camp in Hoy that 'The only regular visitors we had, the twelve or so of us, were the dispatch rider who came with mail and orders about every two days, and the ration lorry which came once a week. The rest of the time the men were left in a battery site set amid miles of emptiness, with just a radio for entertainment.'

This cartoon by 'Strube' appeared in *The Orkney Blast* just before Christmas in 1942, one of many spirited cartoons which appeared in the Orkney garrison newspaper during World War II. (Private collection)

Others were in a worse situation. The same gunner later served as a dispatch rider and visited a two-man outpost served once a week. The men there disliked each other and and he was their only regular contact with the outside world. Another serviceman is reputed to have written his first letter home since being stationed in Orkney:

Dear Mum,
I cannot tell you where I am. I don't know where I am. But where I am there is miles and miles of bugger all.
Love, Ted.

If you had access to Kirkwall, Stromness or even Lyness Naval Base, the situation was markedly different. They boasted cinemas and theatres where well-known acts of stage and screen came to entertain the troops. Gracie Fields and George Formby were regular visitors to Orkney, and some servicemen still recall a memorable concert by the violinist Yehudi Menuhin, 'reminding us of things that were apart from the routine of war'. At Lyness servicemen could visit the NAAFI for a good meal, then see a film, albeit usually an old one. Then there was the bar, where beer was rationed by tickets – three per man.

Naturally, this system was open to barter and misuse, as hundreds of soldiers, sailors and marines all vied with each other to drink as much as they could during their one weekly visit. 'The result was something like a Hogarth print; but frequently the native ability of sailors to entertain emerged, and before long spaces were cleared and various ships put on impromptu shows.'

Kirkwall was the centre of civilization. It had real hotels and restaurants, real pubs and a real cinema. One Wren also remembered the shops: 'Kirkwall's one main street was like Bond Street to us. ... We'd start at one end of the main street and be in and out of the shops till we reached the other.' Other less fortunate members of the garrison were a little more cynical. One later claimed: 'I heard on good authority that there was entertainment for the troops in the Orkneys, provided by ENSA, even great names like dear ole Tommy Handley. But small searchlight units saw none; we had to be satisfied with our battered dartboards and greasy packs of cards.'

For a few servicemen, their abiding memories of Orkney were happy ones. They were the ones able to revel in the rare beauty of the place, and in the nature surrounding them. One young Wren remembered that:

The colours of Orkney are so soft and lovely that there seems to be a sort of pearly radiance over everything. I have heard Orkney called the Magnetic North, and that's how it appeared to me. There was a kind of mystical light, a feeling I have never found anywhere else. And for all there were the normal noises of a busy Naval base and port, there always seemed to be an odd quiet over the land, broken only by the soft lap of water.

Another Wren recalled that: 'To me this lonely outpost was sheer magic. I adored those black isolated moors, and rolling treeless hills, and sudden unexpected lochs. … My main memory is of the sheer beauty of the lonely islands, the lovely colours of the hills, the rare wild flowers, and seabirds, and seals which followed me round my coastal walks, and above all the kindly, friendly local crofters.' A soldier described the long summer nights, where you could read a book outside at midnight. He added: 'The hardships were relative – later service in Burma made me realise this – and taken all round they were outweighed by memories of the wind, wild seas, terns diving over the rocks, and above all, the friendly Orcadians.'

Finally there was the reason the garrison was in Orkney in the first place during two world wars – Scapa Flow, and the British Fleet. Long after the end of World War I, serviceman Percy Ingleby remembered seeing the fleet in all its glory:

I recall how, one Sunday evening, I stood alone 800 feet above the Flow, on the top of Ward Hill, familiar to all who know Scapa, and gazed at the Fleet lying at anchor below. At ten o'clock, four bells rang out from one of the ships, followed by the 'Still'. Immediately, from the quarterdeck of every ship in the Fleet, came the sound of the Sunset bell, with perfect timing. The memory of the clarity of that call, as it came over the silent sea, stirs my heart even now. As I write about it after 50 years, and realize the likelihood that it may never be heard again, tears spring to my eyes, and many others must feel as I do, who knew Scapa in those days, when Britain's sea-power was spoken of with pride and was a reality accepted by the whole world.

SCAPA FLOW AT WAR

During World War I enemy U-boats posed the only real threat to Scapa Flow. Unfortunately, when the war began, the anti-submarine defences of the base were minimal consisting of a fishing net strung between buoys as a makeshift anti-submarine boom and lookouts searching for periscopes.

U-boats were spotted off Scapa Flow during these first months of the war, but it was only on 23 November 1914 that an attempt was made to penetrate

The German press called the U-boat commander Korvettenkapitän Günther Prien the 'Bull of Scapa Flow' after U-47 penetrated the defences of the base in October 1939 and sank HMS Royal Oak. (Stratford Archive)

These sailors from the *Royal Oak* were photographed on board the drifter *Daisy II* on 13 October 1939, as they headed towards Scapa Pier to savour the delights of wartime Kirkwall. Two out of every three crewmen from the battleship were killed the following day. (Stratford Archive)

the anchorage. Kapitänleutnant von Hennig in *U-18* submerged in the Pentland Firth and entered Hoxa Sound. However, when he encountered the makeshift anti-submarine boom stretched between Roan Head and Hunda he decided to give up on the attempt. In truth he could probably have dived beneath it. The current disoriented him and he came to periscope depth off Hoxa Head, only to be rammed by a converted trawler. He subsequently ran aground on the Pentland Skerries, at which point he scuttled his boat.

This was the last serious German attempt to penetrate the defences of Scapa Flow until the last weeks of the war. By that time the anti-submarine defences were formidable, and included induction loops, guard loops and controlled minefields. On 28 October 1918, Oberleutnant Emsmann in *U-116* decided to enter Scapa Flow through Hoxa Sound. He hoped to sneak in beneath a British warship. However, at 8pm the hydrophone station on Stanger Head detected his approach. The defenders switched on the searchlights, and the guard loops. Then at 11.30pm Emsmann's periscope was sighted at the entrance to Pan Hope, just south of Roan Head. That meant that the U-boat was almost on top of the controlled minefield. Minutes later the galvanometer in Roan Read flickered as the U-boat passed over the guard loop in front of the minefield. The order was given to activate the controlled minefield, which was then detonated. *U-116* went down with all hands, leaving a twisted wreck on the seabed. She had the distinction of being the last U-boat casualty of the war, and the only one to be destroyed by a minefield controlled from the shore.

When World War II began in September 1939 Scapa Flow was almost as poorly defended as it had been in 1914, although this time at least anti-submarine booms were in place across the two main entrances. Blockships

During a bombing raid on 16 March 1940 around 50 German bombs were released over this cluster of houses at the Brig of Waithe near Stromness. One of the cottages was hit, killing its occupant James Isbister. He was one of the first British civilian air raid casualties of the war. (Stratford Archive)

sealed off the small eastern channels, while more blockships were due to be scuttled to seal off these channels completely. That September the Luftwaffe conducted reconnaissance flights over the anchorage, and naval analysts discovered that one of these entrances – Kirk Sound – wasn't completely sealed. It was just possible that a daring U-boat commander could thread his way through the blockships, and so penetrate the defences of Scapa Flow. The man chosen to make the attempt was Korvettenkapitän Günther Prien, who commanded *U-47*.

By the afternoon of 13 October 1939, *U-47* was lying submerged off the eastern coast of Orkney as her commander waited for darkness to fall. This still wouldn't provide much cover though, as it was an exceptionally clear night, and the aurora borealis (northern lights) lit up the sky. At 7.15pm the U-boat came to the surface, and Prien set a course for Kirk Sound. By 11.30pm he was in Holm Sound, with the high tide working in his favour, and he steered between the small island of Lamb Holm and the Mainland, evading the blockships set there to prevent just such a passage.

Prien then headed westwards towards the main anchorage but found it empty, the fleet having sailed the previous evening. He then turned northwards towards Scapa Bay and, shortly before 1am, he spotted a battleship lying just over a kilometre off the eastern shore. She was anchored off Gaitnip, where her anti-aircraft guns were able to cover Kirkwall in case the town was attacked. Prien approached the battleship from the south, until he was within 3,600m (4,000 yards) of his target. He fired four torpedoes, although one failed to launch. Although he didn't score any hits, at 1.04am there was a small explosion forward, possibly from a torpedo striking the anchor cable. On board the battleship – HMS *Royal Oak* – it was thought that the explosion was an internal one, from one of the forward inflammable materials store. While the captain and the duty watch investigated, the rest of the battleship's crew went back to sleep.

Meanwhile Prien had turned his U-boat around and fired one of his two stern tubes. Once again the torpedo missed. Prien calmly steamed away to the

south, then reversed course once the bow tubes had been reloaded. At 1.15pm he fired three more torpedoes. This time there were no mistakes, and two or three of them hit the starboard side of the battleship. A survivor described what happened: 'Then, just 13 minutes after the first explosion, came three more sickening, shattering thuds abaft us on the starboard side. Each explosion rocked the ship alarmingly, all lights went out, and she at once took on a list of about 25°.' Eight minutes later the battleship rolled over and sank, taking 833 men down with her.

Prien steered *U-47* back towards Kirk Sound at full speed, leaving the anchorage in an uproar. Prien and *U-47* returned safely to a hero's welcome in Germany.

If anything good came of the tragedy it was that the War Office and the Admiralty finally realized that Scapa Flow's defences were inadequate, a point

F SCAPA FLOW: THE SINKING OF THE *ROYAL OAK*

The spread of three torpedoes which sank HMS *Royal Oak* were fired at 1.13hrs, at a range of a little over 3,000m (3,300 yards). At that distance the torpedoes took almost three minutes to reach their target. On board *U-47* two or possibly three explosions were recorded at 1.15hrs, and a blinding light illuminated the British battleship, followed a few seconds water by a shock wave. A column of fire rose and then vanished, to be replaced by a plume of smoke. Before Korvettenkapitan Prien gave the orders to turn

away and begin the U-boat's escape from Scapa Flow, he saw that the *Royal Oak* was listing heavily, and was obviously sinking. Two nautical miles beyond her lay another ship – the seaplane tender HMS *Pegasus* – and signal lamps began flashing on board her, presumably reporting the attack to other warships in the anchorage. During Prien's exit from Scapa Flow, he evaded a destroyer and searchlights to make good his escape. By 2.15hrs *U-47* had reached the comparative safety of the open sea.

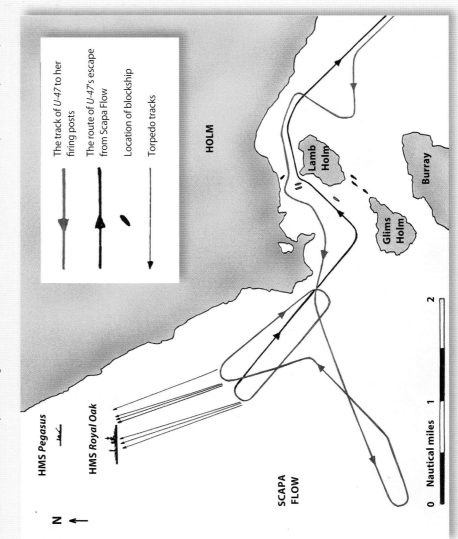

The remains of the blockship SS *Reginald* lie beside Barrier No. 3, between Glims Holm and Burray. The Clyde-built motor schooner was scuttled in 1915. The wreck is now used as a convenient shelter for Burray lobster fishermen. (Author's collection)

which was reinforced just four days after the *Royal Oak* disaster, when the first air attack was launched against the fleet in Scapa Flow.

At dawn on 17 October 1939 four Ju 88 medium bombers attacked the battleship HMS *Iron Duke*, which was anchored off Lyness. She was then serving as the floating base headquarters. She was damaged and was towed onto a nearby sandbank, to prevent her from sinking. She remained beached for the rest of the war.

That afternoon the bombers returned, but no ships were hit, although one bomb exploded near the oil tanks of Lyness – the first bomb to land on British soil. The fleet promptly withdrew to safer bases. In the months that followed the Orkney defences were strengthened, until in March 1940 it was deemed a secure anchorage, and the Home Fleet returned to Scapa. Amongst the other improvements was the provision of anti-aircraft guns, as Scapa Flow was vulnerable to air attack. These air defences were put to the test within weeks of the fleet's return.

At dusk on 16 March about 15 German medium bombers attacked two targets – the warships at anchor in Scapa Flow, and the new Fleet Air Arm airfield at Hatston, near Kirkwall. The cruiser HMS *Norfolk* was holed by a near miss and nine of her crew were killed. This was the raid that resulted in Orkney's first civilian casualty, killed by a cluster of bombs that were dropped near the Brig of Waithe near Stromness. This raid highlighted problems with the coordination of anti-aircraft fire, and the lack of warning provided by radar. The result was the development of the 'Scapa Barrage', a defensive wall of flak designed to keep attacking aircraft away from the main anchorage.

The Luftwaffe returned on 8 April, when 24 medium bombers (a mixture of Ju 88s and Heinkel He IIIs) attacked the booms and other defences of Hoxa Sound. No hits were scored, but it was claimed that seven German bombers were shot down. This time the British had ample warning of the attack, as the anti-aircraft cruiser HMS *Curlew* used her radar to detect the enemy before they reached Orkney.

This raid was timed as a distraction, covering the German invasion of Denmark and Norway. Another raid was expected, and this materialized at dusk on 10 April, when 60 German Ju 88s and He IIIs attacked in two waves, one from the east, the other from the south-east. Both waves approached at just under 3,000m (10,000ft), but were met by the full force of the 'Scapa Barrage'. Only one wave of 20 aircraft penetrated the wall of flak, and once again their bombs were aimed at the Hoxa Boom defences. No hits were scored, although the heavy cruiser HMS *Suffolk* suffered minor damage. At least five of the attacking aircraft were shot down, although intelligence later reported that several damaged German aircraft never made it back to their bases.

That was the last major air attack on Scapa Flow, as the Germans had realized that the air defences around Scapa Flow were now too strong to make another large-scale attack viable. However, a half-hearted raid on 24 April tried to probe its way around the barrage, with only five aircraft actually penetrating the defences to reach Scapa Flow itself. No hits were scored. From that point on the Germans limited themselves to mine-laying and reconnaissance missions, and even these were considered dangerous as the radar defences and fighter cover around Orkney meant that these operations were costly. The Luftwaffe and the Kriegsmarine never repeated these early war attacks as, rightly enough, they considered an attack on Scapa Flow to be a near-suicidal proposition. Consequently the Home Fleet now had a refuge that was safe from German attack. While it mightn't have seemed like it at the time, the men of the Orkney garrison played a vital strategic role that helped ensure the containment and ultimately the defeat of Nazi Germany. The provision of this all-important safe haven for the Royal Navy was the ultimate achievement of the Scapa Flow defences.

THE AFTERMATH OF WORLD WAR II

The threat to Orkney receded a little after the German invasion of the Soviet Union in April 1941, as enemy resources were diverted elsewhere. While Scapa Flow served as a base for those Royal Navy warships engaged in protecting the Arctic convoys, for the rest of the garrison it must have seemed as if the crisis had passed by the winter of 1941/42. Still, it wasn't until the summer of 1943 that the first of two major reductions in the Orkney garrison took place, as first the searchlight batteries were withdrawn, followed by many of the anti-aircraft guns. The searchlights had largely been rendered redundant by the introduction of radar fire control for the HAA batteries, while by 1944 the guns themselves were needed around London to counter the new threat provided by German V1 rockets. The barrage balloons were the next to go, destined to augment the defences of London and the Channel ports. Many of the Army units defending Orkney were withdrawn amid the preparations for D-Day, while several coastal defence batteries were rendered redundant by the building of the Churchill Barriers.

The Italian Chapel was built on Lamb Holm by Italian prisoners of war, whose camp was located on the small island during World War II. This impressive little chapel was constructed around the shell of a corrugated iron 'Nissen hut'. Inside the chapel the walls were (and still are) decorated with religious images painted by the prisoners. (Author's collection)

Following the surrender of Germany on 8 May 1945 the dismantling of the Orkney defences began in earnest, although many servicemen remained there for several months before they were demobbed. There were still the Italian prisoner-of-war camps to guard, and while work began on the demolition of camps and defences, the bulk of the fleet headed south or set course for the waters of the Far East. OSDef was reduced to a brigade-sized command, and then turned into a battalion-sized garrison before being disbanded. The guns were removed from their positions and sent south into storage or to the scrapyards, while one by one the airfields were dismantled. The business of clearing the minefields, or turning land back to civilian use, would take several years to complete, but gradually the last few members of the garrison returned home and sheep and cattle grazed amid the gun emplacements.

The official end came on 29 March 1959, when the white ensign was hauled down at Lyness, and the base was closed. It had been the last operational remnant of a wartime garrison that had once exceeded 40,000 men and women. Once more, Scapa Flow was left to the Orcadians, although the derelict remains of gun batteries, Nissen huts, blockships and air-raid shelters still dotted the Orkney landscape, a crumbling but potent reminder of the time when Orkney had been the best-defended naval base in wartime Europe.

G LYNESS NAVAL BASE, 1942

Lyness served two main purposes. It was the official headquarters of the Royal Navy – the base known as HMS *Prosperine*. This base included theatres, cinemas, canteens, recreation facilities and all the other necessities of garrison life. A key part of the facility was the supply of fuel oil to the Home Fleet, and this was housed in a series of large storage tanks.

The waterfront was dominated by a quay (nicknamed the 'Golden Wharf'), which is still under construction in this view. Lyness was also the maintenance base for the boom defences of Scapa Flow, and the home port of the small fleet of drifters, repair ships and boom defence vessels which kept the boom defences operating.

Churchill Barrier No. 3,
spanning Weddel Sound
between the islands of Glims
Holm (seen in the distance) and
Burray. As Italian POWs were
forbidden to work on defensive
structures, the road built on
top turned these anti-shipping
barriers into a project designed
to improve communications
between the islands.
(Author's collection)

THE DEFENCES OF SCAPA FLOW TODAY

While for decades the Orcadians might have cursed the remnants of Scapa Flow's wartime defences as blight on the landscape, today these remains are regarded with more tolerance. Since the end of World War II these sites reverted to civilian use, and some buildings were even used as homes, most notably at Hatston near Kirkwall, where the buildings of HMS *Sparrowhawk* were used as temporary housing by the local council, and remained in use until the 1970s. Elsewhere farmers used wartime buildings as farm steadings, while remote searchlight emplacements and gun batteries became useful livestock shelters. Today traces of these defences can be seen all over Orkney, making a landscape as rich in wartime history as it is in Neolithic pre-history.

Many of the coastal gun batteries have survived virtually intact, although the camps which once supported them have long since been dismantled. Today their empty searchlight positions, gun emplacements and battery observation posts provide the most vivid reminder of Orkney's wartime past. Of these the battery sites at Stanger Head, Roan Head and Neb in Flotta, Hoxa and Balfour in South Ronaldsay and Rerwick Head in Tankerness have been opened to public access, allowing ramblers to explore their remains. The Houton Battery is also easily accessible, while the Links Battery outside Stromness now lies beside a road leading to a popular coastal viewpoint over Hoy Sound.

Most other battery sites, such as Carness, Holm, Burray and Deerness, are on private land, and visitors should ask permission from the local farmer before exploring the sites. The Ness Battery outside Stromness is still owned by the Ministry of Defence, who deny the public access to the site. Some of these batteries are no longer safe to enter, particularly those at Hoxa and Carness, where the past seven decades of Orkney weather have done little to improve the condition of the concrete emplacements.

Lyness Naval Base is now the site of a small museum, and the wharf there serves as Hoy's main ferry terminal. While traces of the base can still be seen, and several original buildings survive, the area has a melancholy air, as those buildings that remain stand amid the concrete scars of the once-bustling naval base. All but one of the oil storage tanks have been dismantled, although it at least has been preserved and has now been ingeniously transformed into part

The remains of the blockship SS *Lycia*, which was sunk in Skerry Sound between Lamb Holm and Glims Holm in 1939. While these blockships sealed off most of the small, eastern channels into Scapa Flow, in October 1939 *U-47* still managed to pick her way past the blockships in Kirk Sound and enter the naval anchorage which lay beyond (Author's collection).

of the museum. In the early 1970s the nearby island of Flotta was transformed when it became the site of an oil terminal, the terminus of a pipeline running from the oilfields of the North Sea. However, traces of Flotta's wartime remains still exist, including the bare walls of the garrison theatre, and the intriguing remains of the rocket batteries on Roan Head. Oil tankers now ride at anchor in Scapa Flow where once the main fleet anchorage once lay, immediately to the north of Flotta. Few of the tanker crews would realize that one of the buoys in the anchorage marks the last resting place of HMS *Vanguard*, while a few miles to the north-east another buoy lies over the hulk of HMS *Royal Oak*.

While the 6in. gun emplacements on Hoxa Head dating from World War I were built over in 1939, these 4in. emplacements a little to the north were left untouched. They are built in a similar manner to the Ness Battery near Stromness. (Author's collection)

This emplacement at Rerwick Head in Tankerness once housed a 6in. BL Mark VII gun, one of two large gun positions in the battery. The 6in. guns were installed in March 1941, replacing two 4.7in. QF pieces which had been installed in the battery after being removed from the aged dreadnought HMS *Iron Duke*. (Author's collection)

Ness Battery No. 3, overlooking Hoy Sound just outside Stromness. Today the three 4in. gun positions dating from World War I are incorporated into part of the rough of Stromness Golf Club. (Author's collection)

These aren't the only warships to lie in Scapa Flow. Today the remains of the German High Seas Fleet, which was scuttled in 1919, is one of the most popular wreck diving attractions in the world, and every year these sites are visited by thousands of scuba divers. The wrecks of three battleships – the *König, Kronprinz Wilhelm* and *Markgraf* – and four cruisers – *Brummer, Karlsruhe, Köln* (II) and *Dresden* (II) – are all that remain of the age of the dreadnought. Actually, that isn't quite true. Today the wrecks constitute one of the world's best reserves of non-radioactive steel, as metal from the ships doesn't contain the radioactive isotopes found in post-1945 steel. As a result elements of 'Scapa Steel' were used in the construction of the space probe *Voyager*, which means that a small remnant of the dreadnought era still has an important place in mankind's technological quest.

The military airfields of Orkney have long gone, and while few traces of Skeabrae remain the control tower of Twatt still stands sentinel over an airfield that has now been turned over to pasture. Hatston is now an

industrial estate and cruise ship terminal, although visitors can still find traces of its tarmac runways and fighter dispersal bays towards its western edge. As a child the author used to launch sailing dinghies from the Hatston slipway where Walrus seaplanes were once brought ashore, and this crumbling concrete ramp is one of the few remaining traces of the old airfield that still remains in use today. By contrast, Grimsetter airfield to the south-east of Kirkwall was turned over to civilian use, and is now the site of Kirkwall Airport. As late as the early 1970s the airport buildings were adapted from wartime Nissen huts, but today a new terminal building stands in their place, and few traces remain of the old wartime airfield, save the odd grass-covered fighter dispersal bay or overgrown air-raid shelter on the coastal fringes of the modern airport.

Today few Orcadians can imagine life without the Churchill Barriers, providing access between the Orkney Mainland and the charming south isles of Burray and South Ronaldsay. Like Stromness in the West Mainland, the small village of St Margaret's Hope in South Ronaldsay is now a major ferry terminal, linking Orkney to the mainland of Scotland. The route takes the ferry through the once heavily defended waters of Hoxa Sound, beneath

Since the building of Churchill Barrier No. 4 the 1,017-ton steamer SS *Carron*, which was sunk as a blockship in Water Sound in 1940 has gradually been covered by sand. The first picture taken in 1972 shows the author (left) playing on the wreck. The second picture of the author and his father Peter Konstam was taken in 1993, by which time the sand had reached the level of the upper superstructure. The third shows only a few feet of mast remaining above the sand. (Author's collection)

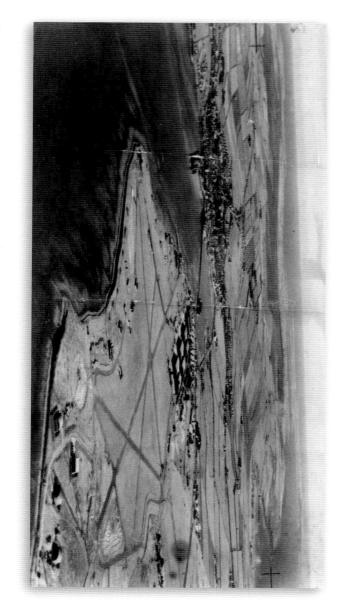

Kirkwall, the principal town in Orkney, from an aerial photograph taken during World War II. In the foreground is HMS *Sparrowhawk*, the Royal Naval Air Station at Hatston, while the masts of the Netherbutton radar station at Netherbutton can be seen in the right middle distance. On the far right is Scapa Bay, the most northerly arm of Scapa Flow. (Orkney Library & Archives)

the now-silent gun batteries of Hoxa and Stanger heads and the last resting place of the *U-116*. In fact it is almost impossible to approach Orkney by sea without passing the empty mouths of gun batteries.

Once passengers land at St Margaret's Hope the drive to Kirkwall takes less than half an hour, taking them across the concrete block-lined Churchill Barriers, the last of which crosses Kirk Sound, where *U-47* stole silently into Scapa Flow on that October night some 70 years ago. Overlooking Kirk Sound is the Italian Chapel, the last remnant of the Italian prisoner-of-war camp on Lamb Holm, one of two such camps in the South Isles and the home of the men who worked on the barriers. Today it is a small Catholic chapel, lovingly restored by former prisoners, and a moving symbol of wartime tribulations and achievement. The rusting remains of blockships still lie close to the barriers, although in many cases the build-up of sand or the decay of salt water have made them far less impressive than they once were. However, they still block the eastern approaches to Scapa Flow, overlooked by the remains of gun emplacements and dwarfed by the Churchill Barriers, which remain the most impressive, as well as the most practical modern reminder of Orkney's wartime past.

Museums and other attractions

Scapa Flow Visitor Centre & Museum, the Old Pumping Station, Lyness, Hoy
Built inside the old wartime oil pumping station and the one surviving oil fuel tank at Lyness, the museum traces the story of wartime Scapa Flow using displays and exhibits, while the tank itself now provides a setting for a large object display area and a film theatre where the history of Scapa Flow is explained.
Open throughout the year.

Orkney Museum, Tankerness House, Broad Street, Kirkwall
Contains displays about 5,000 years of Orkney history, including the impact of both world wars on the community.
Open throughout the year.

Stromness Museum, 52 Alfred Street, Stromness
The museum contains an extensive series of exhibits on Scapa Flow, with a particular emphasis on the scuttling of the German High Seas Fleet. Open throughout the year.

Wireless Museum, Kirkwall, Kiln Corner, Junction Road, Kirkwall
A small but fascinating private museum, tracing the story of wartime communications in Orkney, and containing important wartime memorabilia. Opening times vary.

FURTHER READING

Bowman, Gerald, *The Man who bought a Navy* (London: Harrap, 1964)

Brown, Malcolm, and Patricia Meehan, *Scapa Flow: the reminiscences of men and women who served in Scapa Flow in the two World Wars* (London: Allen Lane Publishing, 1968)

Dorman, Jeff, *Orkney Coast Batteries, 1914–1956* (Kirkwall: The Orcadian, 1996)

Esson, G. L., *Gas Masks and Ration Books: Wartime in South Ronaldsay and Burray* (Orkney: self-published, 2007)

Guy, John, *Orkney Islands: World War One and Two Defences. A Survey* (Edinburgh: RCAHMS, 1993)

Hewison, W. S., *Scapa Flow in War & Peace* (Kirkwall: Bellavista Publications, 1995)

—— *This Great Harbour Scapa Flow* (Edinburgh: Birlinn Publishing, 2005)

Korganoff, Alexander, *The Phantom of Scapa Flow* (London: Ian Allen, 1974)

Lamb, Gregor, *Sky over Scapa, 1939–1945* (Kirkwall: Bellavista Publications, 2007)

Lavery, Brian, *Maritime Scotland* (London: Historic Scotland, 2001)

Macdonald, Catherine M., and E. L. McFarland, *Scotland and the Great War* (Edinburgh: Tuckwell Press, 1999)

Macdonald, Rod, *Dive Scapa Flow* (Edinburgh: Mainstream Publishing, 2007)

Miller, James, *Scapa : Britain's Famous Wartime Naval Base* (Edinburgh: Birlinn Publishing, 2000)

Rollo, D., *The History of the Orkney and Shetland Volunteers and Territorials, 1793–1958* (Lerwick: The Shetland Times, 1958)

Schroder, Virginia, *Bloody Orkney? Orkney during World War II as experienced by some of the men and women stationed there* (Kirkwall: Bellavista Publications, 2006)

Snyder, Gerald S., *The Royal Oak Disaster* (London: Presidio Press, 1978)

Thomson, W. P. L., *History of Orkney* (Edinburgh: Mercat Press, 1987)

Turner, David, *Last Dawn: The Royal Oak Tragedy at Scapa Flow* (Glendaruel, Argyll: Argyll Publishing 2008)

Van der Vat, Dan, *The Grand Scuttle: the sinking of the German fleet at Scapa Flow, 1919* (Edinburgh: Birlinn Publishing, 2003)

Weaver, H. J., *Nightmare at Scapa Flow: The truth about the sinking of the Royal Oak* (Edinburgh: Birlinn Publishing, 2008)

Wood, Lawson, *The Bull and the Barriers: The Wrecks of Scapa Flow* (Kirkwall: NPI Media, 2000)

APPENDIX

Bloody Orkney (Anon) first published in *The Orkney Blast*:

This bloody town's a bloody cuss
No bloody trains, no bloody bus,
And no one cares for bloody us
In bloody Orkney.

The bloody roads are bloody bad,
The bloody folks are bloody mad,
They'd make the brightest bloody sad,
In bloody Orkney.

All bloody clouds, and bloody rains,
No bloody kerbs, no bloody drains,
The Council's got no bloody brains,
In bloody Orkney.

Everything's so bloody dear,
A bloody bob, for bloody beer,
And is it good? – no bloody fear,
In bloody Orkney.

The bloody 'flicks' are bloody old,
The bloody seats are bloody cold,
You can't get in for bloody gold
In bloody Orkney.

The bloody dances make you smile,
The bloody band is bloody vile,
It only cramps your bloody style,
In bloody Orkney.

No bloody sport, no bloody games,
No bloody fun, the bloody dames
Won't even give their bloody names
In bloody Orkney;

Best bloody place is bloody bed,
With bloody ice on bloody head,
You might as well be bloody dead,
In bloody Orkney.

The Orkney Garrison (OSDef), May 1940

OSDef (Maj. Gen. Kemp) HQ: Stromness

Anti-aircraft defences

58th AA Brigade (Col. Hancocks) HQ: Lynnfield, Kirkwall
70th HAA Rgt. (Lt. Col. Bateson) Hobbister, Orphir
comprising 211, 212, 216 & 309 HAA Btys. (3.7in. & 4.5in.)
attached: 39th LAA Bty. (Maj. Rowat) Stromness
59th AA Brigade (Brig. Gen. Peck) HQ: Melsetter, Hoy
64th HAA Rgt. (Lt. Col. Anderson) HQ: Roeberry, Hoy
comprising 178, 179, 180 & 268 HAA Btys. (all 3.7in.)
95th HAA Rgt. (Lt. Col. Lawrence) HQ: South Walls, Hoy
comprising 204, 226 & 293 HAA Btys. (all 3.7in.)
attached: 142nd LAA Bty. (Maj. Perry) Lyness, Hoy

Coastal batteries

Fixed Defences Command (Lt. Col. Cook) Ness Battery, Stromness
191st Heavy Bty. (Maj. Weigall) Ness Battery, Stromness (later 534th Coastal Rgt.)
198th Heavy Bty. (Maj. Moar) Stanger Head Battery, Flotta (later 533rd Coastal Rgt.)
199th Heavy Bty. (Maj. Buist) Rerwick Head Battery, Tankerness (later 536th Coastal Rgt.)
attached: Orkney Fortress Royal Engineers (Maj. Linklater – later Eric Linklater the novelist)

Searchlight batteries

61st Searchlight Rgt. (Lt. Col. Valentine) St. Margaret's Hope, South Ronaldsay
432nd S/L Bty. (Major Pilkington) – 12 sites in Burray and Flotta
433rd S/L Bty. (Major Molyneux) – 18 sites in South Ronaldsay

434th S/L Bty. (Major Ashburner) – 24 sites in Hoy

62nd Searchlight Rgt. (Lt. Col. Whitehead) Orphir

435th S/L Bty. (Major Rainford) – 18 sites in West Mainland

436th S/L Bty. (Major Buckley) – 18 sites in Kirkwall and Orphir

437th S/L Bty. (Major Baines) – 18 sites in East Mainland

Garrison troops

7th Bn., Gordon Highlanders (Lt. Col Hunter-Blair) HQ: Kirkwall companies stationed in Holm, Netherbutton, Stromness

attached: 12th Bn. Highland Light Infantry (1 Company): Kirkwall

3rd Bn. Cameron Highlanders (1 Company): Kirkwall

Royal Engineers (Lt. Col. Baillie) HQ: Stromness Comprising 274th & 276th Field Coys. (Stromness), 279th Field Coy. (South Ronaldsay), 275th Field Coy. (Kirkwall), plus assorted

attached workshop, bomb disposal and stevedore units.

Pioneer Corps (Lt. Col. Duncan) HQ: Ness Battery, with detachments in Kirkwall, Stromness, Hoy, St Margaret's Hope and the West Mainland

152nd Field Rgt., A Bty., RA (Kirkwall)

Royal Signals (Capt. Lothian) Stromness

Service Units

Royal Army Service Corps (Lt. Col. Clarkson) Stromness

Ordnance Corps (Maj. Larmour) HQ: Stromness, with detachments in Stromness, Kirkwall, Hoy and South Ronaldsay attached: Mobile Laundry (Kirkwall)

Royal Army Medical Corps (Lt. Col. Wade) HQ: Stromness

Military Hospital (Kirkwall)

Skin Disease Hospital (Dounby)

RN Hospital (Houton)

No. 1 Field Hospital (Orphir)

No. 2 Field Hospital (Stromness)

No. 3 Field Hospital (Longhope)

Ness Camp, part of the Ness Battery, photographed from 'The Citadel' hill outside Stromness. The battery was built in 1939 on the site of a World War I emplacement, overlooking Hoy Sound, and the westerly approaches to Scapa Flow. (Author's collection)

INDEX